AN EDUCATIONAL PLATFORM
for the
PUBLIC SCHOOLS

by George H. Reavis and Carter V. Good

FACSIMILE EDITION

Published by
Phi Delta Kappa Educational Foundation

Cover design by
Peg Caudell

Phi Delta Kappa Educational Foundation
408 North Union Street
Post Office Box 789
Bloomington, Indiana 47402-0789
U.S.A.

Printed in the United States of America

Library of Congress Catalog Card Number 96-70321
ISBN 0-87367-492-8

Preface

TO THE FACSIMILE EDITION

This book is a facsimile edition of the first book published by the Phi Delta Kappa Educational Foundation.

Written by George H. Reavis, who established the foundation in 1966, and Carter V. Good, another well-known educator, *An Educational Platform for the Public Schools,* published in 1968, sets forth a basic and enduring educational philosophy. While many of the curriculum specifics in this work will seem dated to modern readers, the essence of this small book is sound and timeless.

At the creation of the PDK Educational Foundation, George Reavis articulated a vision of the foundation's work:

> The purpose of the Phi Delta Kappa Educational Foundation is to contribute to a better understanding of (1) the nature of the educative process, and (2) the relation of education to human welfare.

Reavis viewed this purpose in a larger sense as shaping public policy through understanding. Echoing the sentiments of Thomas Jefferson, Reavis wrote:

> In our democracy public policy is determined by popular will, and popular will is based upon popular understanding. Our governmental (and educational) policy can be no better in the long run than our popular understanding.

In addition to offering this facsimile edition as a fitting recognition of the 30th anniversary of the Phi Delta Kappa Educational Foundation, we take this opportunity to offer this book as a work worthy of being read and reflected upon by a new generation in a new era.

Not long ago, John F. Jennings wrote in another small book published by the Phi Delta Kappa Educational Foundation that:

> Today, some Americans seem to be losing faith in the public schools. When discussion turns to the quality of education, it is not uncommon for a friend or neighbor to suggest that the problems of the public schools could be solved by school choice, education vouchers, privatization, home schooling, or some other plan to shift funding and responsibility for education to the private sector. In an age when Americans have begun to question one of the most fundamental elements of society, the public schools, it is useful — indeed necessary — to review why those schools were created in the first place. (*Do We Still Need Public Schools?* 1996)

In order to stimulate such a review, Phi Delta Kappa International recently took steps to initiate a public dialogue about the need for and role of public schools in American education — in American life — through a series of public forums and informative publications. This facsimile edition of *An Educational Platform for the Public Schools* provides an appropriate historical perspective and supports that initiative.

Donovan R. Walling
Editor of Special Publications
Phi Delta Kappa Educational Foundation

1957-1968

An Educational Platform for the

Public Schools

A DECADE OF CHANGE

By George H. Reavis and Carter V. Good

A Publication of the Phi Delta Kappa Educational Foundation

Copyright 1968 by Phi Delta Kappa, Inc.

Eighth and Union

Bloomington, Indiana 47401

PREFACE

This is the first in a series of *Phi Delta Kappa Educational Monographs* to be financed by the Phi Delta Kappa Educational Foundation established in 1966 as a result of the generosity of Dr. George H. Reavis. The Foundation Board of Governors plans to issue a series of annual monographs and books which will contribute to a better understanding of (1) the nature of the educative process, and (2) the relations of education to human welfare.

In a leaflet entitled *Intent of the Grantor* (Phi Delta Kappa, 1968), Dr. Reavis has defined this purpose in considerable detail, listing possible titles of such reports and outlining problem areas they should illuminate. The Board of Governors seeks the world's leading authorities to write these reports, which will then be widely distributed among educators and laymen interested in the perennial problems of education.

We are pleased to present, as the first in this series, the following statement of educational policy, written by Dr. Reavis when he was Director of the Editorial Program, World Book Encyclopedia (1948-58), having retired from his work as director of curriculum and instruction, Cincinnati, Ohio, Public Schools. With the statement is a research-based historical commentary and updating by Carter V. Good, long-time dean of Teachers College, University of Cincinnati.

Edgar Dale, Chairman
Board of Governors
Phi Delta Kappa Educational
Foundation

September, 1968

v

Acknowledgments

Several prominent school administrators and professors of administration were asked to comment on the 1957 version of *An Educational Platform* before Dr. Carter Good undertook the historical commentary and updating which accompanies the original text in this publication. Several of these men were among the scores of superintendents who helped Dr. Reavis produce the first consensus statement in the 1950's. A few were seeing the book for the first time.

The remarks and suggestions of this group were of great help in a number of ways. First, they verified the judgment of the Board of Governors of the Phi Delta Kappa Educational Foundation that the Platform should be reprinted. Second, their comments made it obvious that so much had occurred in American education in the one decade since 1957 that a historical treatment and updating would be essential. Finally, their suggestions were of considerable help to Dr. Good as he prepared the commentary which accompanies the Reavis statement.

The educators who responded to our request were: Melvin W. Barnes, Superintendent, Portland, Oregon, Public Schools; M. Lynn Bennion, Superintendent, Salt Lake City, Utah, Schools; Selmer H. Berg, Superintendent (retired), Oakland, California, Public Schools; Floyd T. Christian, Superintendent, Department of Education, State of Florida; Joseph M. Cronin, Assistant Professor of Education, Administrative Career Program, Graduate School of Education, Harvard University; M. L. Cushman, Dean, College of Education, University of North Dakota; William J. Ellena, Deputy Executive Secretary, American Association of School Administrators, Washington, D.C.; Herold C. Hunt, Eliot Professor of Education, Harvard University; Raymond F. McCoy, Dean, Graduate School, Xavier University, Cincinnati, Ohio; Floyd W. Parsons, Superintendent, Little Rock, Arkansas, Public Schools; Lawrence F. Read, Superintendent, Jackson, Michigan, Public Schools; Mendel Sherman, Assistant Director, Audio-Visual Center, Indiana University; James H. Williams, Superintendent, Glendale, California, Unified School District.

It should be noted that Dr. Ellena not only provided useful commentary, he sketched a design which is the basis for the cover of this volume.

Stanley Elam, Editor
Phi Delta Kappa Publications

CONTENTS

PREFACE v

ACKNOWLEDGMENTS vi

SECTION I: INTRODUCTION 1

SECTION II

Educational Platform 4

Purposes and Responsibilities of Education and the

Schools 10

SECTION III

Educational Platform 12

School Organization: Program and Curriculum 17

SECTION IV

Educational Platform 21

Adaptation to Individual Differences: Instructional-

Learning Procedures 35

SECTION V

Educational Platform 45

Administration, Leadership, and the Teacher 46

SECTION VI

Educational Platform 49

The Role of Science and Research: Values and Issues 56

Section I (R)

INTRODUCTION

Underlying every public school system is an educational philosophy, either assumed or expressed. In the absence of clearly defined educational policy, there is sometimes confusion among teachers and administrators and misunderstanding by the public. In this statement the superintendents of certain city school systems attempt to outline and summarize, for their own use, some elements of acceptable educational policy. These superintendents, with the assistance of members of their staffs, have cooperated over a period of years in the development of this Educational Platform.

The American public school system was founded to help maintain and promote the American way of life. Our educational system has grown as America has grown. The way of life it helps to perpetuate and improve has undergone important changes. The responsibilities of citizenship have broadened. The educative process has gradually become better understood. New and increasing demands are made upon the schools. As the role of the schools becomes more important, and the problems more complex and confusing, the need to define educational policy with vision, clarity, and forcefulness cannot be overemphasized.

George H. Reavis, 1957

Section I

INTRODUCTION

An Educational Platform for the Public Schools was conceived by George H. Reavis as a statement of educational policy and was prepared in cooperation with superintendents of city school systems. The 1957 version reproduced here was based on an earlier statement published in 1952, for which the same author served as coordinator. In this volume the 1957 Reavis statement is presented as he wrote it, in italic type. A commentary prepared in 1968 parallels it, printed in roman type.

The 1957 *Educational Platform for the Public Schools* (R*), as a statement of educational policy, has been characterized by many persons as a basically sound philosophy in many respects, particularly in relation to the time when it was written or in historical perspective, and with various possible applications to the problems and issues of today. However, as a consensus of the experience and views of school superintendents a decade ago, along with the synthesis by Reavis, some of these earlier concepts have been outmoded, others are now more highly developed, and yet others present possibilities for future development. Therefore, the crucial social and economic changes of a decade make it essential to update and supplement this document. The updating is in terms of basic principles and research evidence rather than as a detailed manual or handbook of school organization and instruction.

Certain sources have proved especially valuable in reviewing the philosophy, practice, and research of the past decade: the *Review of Educational Research,* the series of booklets under the general title of *What Research Says to the Teacher,* the AERA *Handbook of Research on Teaching,* yearbooks of the National Society for the Study of Education, the *Phi Delta Kappan,* and the comments of a number of persons (selected by the central office of Phi Delta Kappa) on the 1957 Platform.

The updated statement is not intended as a rewrite of the 1957 Platform. Therefore, a particular section of the original platform appears in italic type, with the appropriate section numbers including the symbol (R), followed by the updating in roman type. Sometimes the best we can do is to identify current issues and problems, with the hope that solutions may be found in the years ahead. Cross-reference to the 1957 Platform is by the symbol (R). In certain instances the sequence of paragraphs found in the 1957 statement has been changed in the interest of

---

* For Reavis.

continuity; for example, "Individual Differences" and "Adapting to Individual Differences" now appear in sequence in the italics part of the statement.

Carter V. Good, 1968
University of Cincinnati

PURPOSES OF EDUCATION

Education is preparation for citizenship in its broadest sense. The development of the individual to the limit of his capacity for complete living in our society is the major purpose of education. The home, the school, the church, the community, and many other agencies share in the responsibility for our education. In educating for well-rounded citizenship, the schools are thus not alone in their efforts. Education is a cooperative enterprise.

The school curriculum is given direction by our concept of the good citizen and his educational needs. The responsibility of citizenship was recognized early by the establishment of schools, primarily for literacy. Reading and writing were taught originally to enable the individual to live well with his fellowmen in a free society.

In America our most cherished goal is freedom. In banding together under the Constitution to protect their common interests and govern themselves, our forefathers were unwilling to yield certain individual rights to the government. The first ten amendments to the Constitution were adopted to safeguard important personal rights. From this emphasis on freedom stems our educational program.

Progress toward freedom comes with the development of the discipline and understandings, and the acceptance of the responsibilities, that freedom entails. Among the worthy personal goals for living are an understanding of, and respect for, one's self, including the self-discipline which comes through our moral and spiritual values. The price of freedom is discipline in the character of the individual citizen. This requires a good basic general education.

The Good Citizen

The good citizen must be economically and socially competent. To be economically competent, the citizen must be able to take his place as a producer in our private-enterprise economy. He must be able to produce as much or more in goods and services as he consumes, or otherwise add to the general welfare and thereby help sustain and improve our standard of living. To be socially competent, he must be politically competent and able to live well with his fellows so that life shall mean no less, and may mean more, for his fellows because he is one of them. These two phases of citizenship education (economic and social competence) require a good general education, including a working mastery of the "three R's" and other fundamentals. The ability to read, and to communicate, is equally necessary for successful employment in business and industry and for military service, as well as for everyday living.

The good citizen is informed on local, national, and world affairs and contributes to an informed public opinion. Improvement in transportation and communication has brought the peoples of the earth closer together and increased their interdependence. Our government now has some responsibility for world leadership. A high level of world understanding is necessary for American citizenship. Social competence includes the ability to be not only a good member of a family and a good neighbor but also a participating member of the larger community. Our citizens should understand our way of life and its basic institutions and have a deep-seated devotion to America, based upon a high level of world understanding.

In a totalitarian society in which the state is supreme and public policy is not determined by the popular will, youth needs to be trained merely to believe, obey, and fight. But in our republic with representative government, where popular will determines public policy, it is not enough to teach our citizens what they are to believe, the persons they are to obey, and the things for which they are to fight. Popular government requires straight-thinking citizens who contribute to an informed public opinion that firmly supports sound public policy.

In a democracy, every man is entitled to his own opinion, but no man has the right to be wrong about the facts on which his opinion is based. No man has the right to be ignorant. *He has the responsibility to base his opinion on the best available information. Scholarship is important in a democracy because the quality of a man's thinking depends upon the range, the validity, and the clarity of his ideas; and his character depends largely upon the nature and strength of his ideals. A high level of general education is necessary to perpetuate the American way of life.*

The American Way

Perhaps we should note the American way in more detail. Our democracy stems from the Judeo-Christian heritage, with emphasis on religious freedom and the brotherhood of man. As a philosophy, American democracy is a system of ethics grounded in religion. We recognize the supreme worth and dignity of the individual consistent with the general welfare and the common good.

"We hold these truths to be self-evident: That all men are created equal; that they are endowed by their Creator with certain unalienable rights; that among these are life, liberty, and the pursuit of happiness. That, to secure these rights, governments are instituted among men, deriving their just powers from the consent of the governed." We believe that our people have the right and the capacity to govern themselves.

We have a government of limited powers. We confer certain powers on our federal and state governments, and reserve certain rights for ourselves as individuals. Government thus derives its "just powers from the consent of the governed." The purpose of government is to preserve and promote the exercise of our rights, and to manage our affairs of common concern. Government is a means to these ends rather than an end in itself.

Our government is a republic, defined by the Constitution of the United States. Our republic is a representative government, with popular rule. Public policy is determined by the people, and is expressed through a system of laws and their administration. Our government is organized in three branches with appropriate checks and balances. Our Constitution provides for change through amendment to meet new needs by evolution rather than by revolution.

All men are equal before the law. The rights of minorities are recognized and protected. The members of minority groups are themselves individuals with "unalienable" rights. Minorities must have the opportunity to become the majority in order to continue majority rule. To suppress minorities, or to deny them the opportunity to become the majority, is to abandon popular government.

Self-government assumes an enlightened electorate. Sound public policy requires an informed public opinion. We therefore recognize the great importance of education and the public school system. "Religion, morality, and knowledge being necessary to good government and the happiness of mankind, schools and the means of education shall forever be encouraged." Freedom to learn, with free access to information, and free discussion, with open avenues of communication, are basic essentials of the American way. We believe that "error of opinion may be tolerated where reason is left free to combat it."

Our economy is based upon private enterprise. The ownership of property and the profit motive stimulate the production and distribution of the goods and services necessary to maintain a high standard of living. Our great productive capacity results from the increased competence, resourcefulness, initiative, and industry of our people expressed through the development of new methods and new resources.

Changing Needs

In recent decades important changes have been taking place. Children and youth in large cities have been increasingly deprived of opportunities to participate in many activities outside of school that formerly helped to educate directly for later life. They no longer work alongside their parents in providing food, clothing, and shelter for the family. When children and youth shared more responsibilities with their parents and participated more actively in family affairs, and the family was a more closely knit economic unit, important educational purposes were served by these activities. The normal activities of children were then more closely in line with their later adult life. Today, our children have certain other advantages but they miss, particularly in larger cities, much of this important experience contributing so greatly to their future educational needs.

Furthermore, with each succeeding generation, more persons work for others. Each person today, more than ever before, needs to learn the relationship between his work—and the quality of this work—and the welfare of himself, his family, and his community. The specialization of industry and its removal from the home and neighborhood have other implications for education. Many parents go to work and children are left at home. Children turn for companionship to other children who are similarly separated from their parents. Parents, at work, associate with other adults. Each age level tends to develop its own set of values and cultural patterns, with less opportunity for one age level to influence the other.

Community life is also more affected by forces that do not originate within the community, but rather outside in the state, nation, and world. The schools have a responsibility to help pupils understand and cope with these forces. At appropriate age levels pupils understand the position of each important community organization on vital issues and why that organization takes its particular stand. Where such local organization is a part of a larger organization, the issue should, within the maturity of the pupils, be understood also in its wider relationships.

Moreover, most of the significant additions to our culture reach the people as a whole through the schools. As science continues to add to our knowledge of the universe, as scholars delve more deeply into the past, and as unfolding history itself adds new pages, there is increasingly more to be taught. The hazards of a more dangerous environment have increased the responsibility of the schools for safety education. Thus, as the home and other agencies teach relatively less, and the body of knowledge to be taught grows larger, and as our life becomes more com-

plex, the responsibility for discriminating between the important and less important in education grows greater, and the problem of desirable public school policy becomes more urgent and complex.

RESPONSIBILITIES OF THE SCHOOLS

Formal education began originally with the introduction and wide use of written language. The public schools were established to teach those essentials not taught adequately by other agencies in society. In the beginning the curriculum was limited to reading, writing, and arithmetic; but the kind and amount of education required for complete living have greatly increased. The educational service rendered by the home and some other agencies has declined or changed. As a result, the school curriculum has grown enormously. No other people has ever expected so much of its schools. It is important, therefore, to define clearly the role of the public schools, and continually to review and appraise the educational program.

Threefold Function

The responsibilities of the public schools may be viewed as threefold. The public schools have (1) primary or chief responsibility for some phases of education, (2) partial or shared responsibility for other phases of education, and (3) some responsibility for educational leadership in the community.

1. The public schools have primary or chief responsibility for reading, handwriting, arithmetic, spelling, and the basic essentials of oral and written composition, the social studies (geography, history, and civics), and science. Reading is an important primary responsibility of the schools. Legible handwriting, proficiency in arithmetic for ordinary needs, and the ability to spell one's written vocabulary are also essentials for which the schools accept major responsibility. Certain basic elements of the social studies and science, and a working proficiency in the use of English, are also primary responsibilities of the schools.

2. Responsibility for some other phases of education is shared jointly, and in varying degrees, by the schools and other educational agencies. These shared responsibilities include vocational fitness and certain broad outcomes of general education such as the American way of life, health and safety, scientific attitude of mind, consumer competence, thrift, family living, conservation, the arts, moral and spiritual values, and the worthy use of leisure time.

3. The schools also have some responsibility for helpful counsel and educational leadership in the community. They support and cooperate with other recognized educational agencies in the performance of their established educational functions in order to help provide a well-rounded educational program for the community as a whole.

These three responsibilities of the public schools are not separate. They are closely interrelated and operate concurrently. The schools, however, see each of these functions distinctly and strive to perform all three of them well. Unless the schools perform the first function (primary responsibilities) well, they cannot perform the second one (shared responsibilities) well; and unless they perform each of the first two functions efficiently, they cannot provide helpful counsel and educational leadership in the community. For this reason, the public schools first make sure that they achieve well those things for which they have primary responsibility, but they do this without neglecting their shared responsibilities. At the same time, the schools strive to provide helpful counsel and educational leadership for the community and thus measure up to all three of their important responsibilities.

Section II

PURPOSES AND RESPONSIBILITIES
OF EDUCATION AND THE SCHOOLS

Some of the problems and developments (listed more completely in the last section) that could not be fully or accurately predicted a decade ago relate to: federal programs and issues of decentralization, the tremendous growth of research and knowledge, appropriate allocation of resources to education, greater interdependence between educational institutions and socioeconomic forces, economic interdependence within our own country and abroad, the population explosion, poverty, jobs, housing, health, aging, atomic war, outer space exploration, race and minority groups, integration, civil rights, academic freedom, drugs, sex, "revolt" of the young, urban school systems, and inner-city children.

In view of the critical problems of the decade, it is overly optimistic today to claim that "our educational system has grown as America has grown" (R). A major reason for this lag is the very limited amount of good school-system research, along with the relatively meager support of such research.

The first ten amendments to the federal Constitution were adopted to safeguard important personal rights (R), but the Fourteenth Amendment made the first ten applicable to the states. From this stems our education program, with education a CONCERN of the federal government, but a FUNCTION of the states.

The purposes and principles of education directly involve our value systems (treated more fully in a later section), as well as both political and educational aspects of a working philosophy.

Some social scientists maintain that "preparation for citizenship" (R) is too narrow as terminology and that the broader term "culture" really is involved in this objective. While one objective of education is to assist each individual in becoming a productive and participating member of our society, another major purpose is to help the individual learner know, respect, and become himself as he learns to work with and for others; expressed otherwise, it is development of the individual to the limit of his capacity for complete living in our society. This philosophy requires more effective programs of preservice and in-service education of teachers consistent with the policies and objectives of local school systems, and treatment of program organization, personnel, and school plant as vehicles for attaining the educational purposes.

In more specific terms, the most important objectives and responsibilities of the schools and education include: critical and effective methods of thinking, curiosity and creativity, useful work habits and study skills, constructive social attitudes and relationships, a range of significant interests, appreciation of the fine arts (music, art, literature, and other esthetic experiences), social sensitivity, personal-social adjustment, effective communication and expression, important information and knowledge, physical and mental health, ethics, and a consistent philosophy of life. Both elementary and secondary schools should divest themselves of the overwhelming influence of higher education and orient their policies and programs toward objectives more attainable by the majority of our youth. It is true that a number of these purposes are shared with other social institutions and agencies of the community, and that we are adopting a more manageable conception of the teacher's (and the school's) function. Thus we now concede more readily that other agencies of society must play a major role in achieving social, esthetic, physical, and vocational objectives.

The statement on the characteristics of the "good citizen" should be read with emphasis on "thinking citizens who contribute to an informed public opinion" (R), without any assumption that we teach our future citizens what they are to believe. It may be that this idealistic characterization (*in toto*) of the good citizen is an unrealistic expectation in certain of our population centers of today. Desirable as the goal of enlightenment may be, some philosophers raise a question concerning the concept of "free choice" in relation to the statement that no man has "the right to be ignorant" (R).

We agree, of course, that the basic tenet of the American philosophy is its concern for the worth and dignity of each individual regardless of race, national origin, or creed. With respect to minorities, however, today we have great pressures on society, government, and education through various forms of propaganda and demonstration, involving war, draft cards, black power, student power, etc. Although minorities must have the opportunity, through due process of law, to become the majority, the rights of the majority also must be recognized by minorities.

SCHOOL ORGANIZATION

Although the public school curriculum is basically 8-4, schools in large city systems are usually 6-3-3 in administrative organization. In rural districts administrative organization is often 6-6, sometimes 8-4. The plan of the curriculum and the type of administrative organization that implements it should not be confused. The curriculum of grades seven and eight should be basically the same whether the pupils are in elementary schools, in junior high schools, or in six-year high schools. The administrative organization in a particular school system is sometimes influenced or limited by the geography of the school district, the transportation facilities, and the school buildings available, but these influences should not substantially affect the curriculum.

The Elementary School

The elementary school usually includes the kindergarten and first six grades. These younger children can be taught better when separated from older pupils and organized into easily accessible, separate schools adapted to their special needs. The elementary school provides the basic foundations of general education.

The educational program at any level is determined not only by the immediate present needs of pupils but also by the demands of the days, weeks, months, and years ahead. Although many topics repeat in cycles from grade to grade, the skills, understanding, and attitudes developed in the curriculum are usually most easily built in a definite order. The program in each grade continues the preceding grade and leads to the next with close continuity. The elementary school has a well-planned curriculum.

The Junior High School

The junior high school usually includes grades seven, eight, and nine, organized in separate schools. These early adolescent children can usually be taught better when separated both from the younger children in the grades below and from the more mature adolescents in the grades above. These pupils can also travel farther to school than younger children, and enough of them can be brought to justify the special facilities and the organization to provide a well-rounded program better suited to their interests and needs.

The junior high school, midway in type between that of the elementary school and the senior high school, is planned especially for preadolescents and early adolescents. The transition from the usual self-contained classroom plan of the elementary school to the fully departmentalized organization of the senior high school is made gradually in the junior high school. The transition from the prescribed program in grades seven and eight to a differentiated curriculum in grade nine comes within a school rather than between schools. This is especially helpful in educational and vocational guidance, which is important on this level.

The Senior High School

The senior high school usually includes grades ten, eleven, and twelve, and is organized and administered separately to meet more specifically the needs of older adolescents. The separate organization of the senior high school also permits the concentration of the more expensive and specialized equipment and facilities for these grades into fewer schools.

High schools are no longer selective in their membership. Emphasis is placed upon holding power. As a result, fewer pupils drop out before completing the course. All youths of high school age should be kept in school until they complete a high school program. The high schools are open to all the children of all the people, and provide programs that make their attendance worthwhile.

The Community College

The community (or junior) college is generally considered an extension of the public school system through grades thirteen and fourteen, and is now well established in many parts of the country. The community college continues the general education of youth, prepares for later professional training in higher institutions, and also provides additional vocational education and other terminal courses for students under home supervision during later adolescence.

Adult Education

Provision is usually made for the continuation of education on the adult level. Some adults wish to complete a high school education while working to support themselves and others. Some need to meet naturalization requirements. Other employed adults wish to prepare for promotion in responsibility and remuneration. Some adults desire to become more effective in homemaking and in civic affairs. Some want additional education to meet social and recreational needs, and still others wish to satisfy personal desires for additional knowledge or skills in some particu-

lar field. The provision for adult education, therefore, contributes to per-
sonal, social, economic, and civic competence and is usually included in
the program of large city public school systems.

Vocational Education

Many graduates of senior high schools and junior colleges go directly
into wage-earning pursuits. Some of these pupils, in addition to devoting
much time to general education, take such vocational subjects as stenog-
raphy, office practice, bookkeeping, sales, and other distributive educa-
tion courses. For other pupils, appropriate training for the trades and in-
dustries is provided. In rural communities, vocational agriculture is em-
phasized. For certain other pupils, the fine arts provide both more gen-
eral education and also specific training for vocations in later life.

The vocational program in the public schools includes necessary gen-
eral education and also those types of vocational instruction which can
be more effectively and more economically provided by the schools than
by other agencies. The public schools share responsibility for vocational
education with the home, the community, business, labor, industry, the
farm, and other agencies. Much specialized occupational and technical
training is provided by industry, business, and other agencies, but there
are many fields of employment for which vocational education can and
should be provided by the schools.

Most (usually as much as three-fourths) of the first two years of a voca-
tional program in a four-year high school is devoted to general education.
During the last two years there is usually increased emphasis on prepa-
ration for a wage-earning pursuit, with varying amounts (usually about
one-half) of the time devoted to general education. Vocational compe-
tence requires a working mastery of the "three R's" and other fundamen-
tals. The ability to read, and certain other basic skills, are necessary for
successful employment and for military service. Each worker needs a good
general education.

Preparation for a vocation is planned to terminate not earlier than the
age of employability and at the time the pupil leaves school. The length
and amount of vocational instruction vary with the occupation for which
the instruction is intended. The vocational program is usually based upon
an occasional survey of the community and region, and upon other infor-
mation. The schools make provision for a wide range of individual abili-
ties and future needs of pupils.

Most school systems provide for vocational education in departments
or divisions of comprehensive high schools, but some types of vocational
education that require expensive equipment or other special facilities are

occasionally organized in a single, centrally located, separate school. The community (junior) college, wherever a part of the public school system, usually offers vocational courses. The foregoing principles apply with equal force to planning vocational programs in the community college.

THE CURRICULUM

The curriculum includes all those learning activities provided by the schools for the education of children. In general, the subjects (fields or areas) of study in the kindergarten and first eight grades are common for all children. This is often called the "common school curriculum" because the subjects are common for all pupils. The curriculum of these eight grades includes those elements of our cultural heritage which all citizens should appreciate, acquire, and make a part of themselves; which, in varying degrees, can be profitably taught to all; and which can be more efficiently and economically taught by the schools than by other educational agencies.

In the first six grades all pupils (except perhaps some of the handicapped) study the language arts, the social studies (geography, history, and civics), mathematics, science, art, music, and health, physical education, and safety. To these seven areas, industrial arts and home economics, or other courses in crafts and home arts, are usually added in grades seven and eight.

The curriculum in grades nine through twelve continues these nine fields and usually adds foreign languages and vocational subjects. The program in these grades continues general education for all and provides specialized education for groups. Usually one-half to two-thirds of the curriculum is common for all pupils in grades nine through twelve. These common subjects continue general education and are important regardless of the occupations and avocations the pupils may later follow. General education and specialized education are not separate, but are closely interrelated. Each is an important part of the other.

The major curriculum problems in large high schools stem chiefly from three sources—the wide range of interests and capacities of pupils, the multiplicity of separate courses, and the narrow specialization of subject matter in many of these courses. After a tremendous growth in the number of separate courses in large high schools during the last 50 years, the trend is now definitely toward fewer (and more inclusive) courses, with more pupils taking these fewer, broader courses and with the courses more effectively adapted to the varying capacities and needs of the pupils who take them.

In very small high schools the curriculum is usually too narrow and the teaching assignments too wide, but in large high schools the problems are often the reverse. In large high schools, many courses, narrow in scope and shallow in depth, are being eliminated, and the essentials of these courses transferred to the broader and more substantial courses remaining. Requirements for graduation are being made more specific, and the administration of the guidance program is being emphasized to limit further the scope of the elective system for individual pupils. At the same time, subject matter is being found not in books alone, but increasingly in the lives of pupils or in the community, or created in realistic situations and activities in the classroom, to bring a higher degree of functional realism and vitality to what is taught.

Section III

SCHOOL ORGANIZATION:
PROGRAM AND CURRICULUM

During the past decade certain aspects of school organization and program have undergone considerable change or development, including preschool education (especially federally supported programs), early childhood education, the middle school, the concept of the educational park, area occupational or technical centers for vocational education, the community or "people's" college, adult education, higher education more generally, and the curriculum itself at all levels.

The programs of recent years for curriculum development and innovation have been influenced by rapid advances in technology and automation, the knowledge "explosion," changes in society especially related to integration and the culturally disadvantaged, emphases on subject-centered and discipline-centered content, demands for amplification of curriculum requirements combined with attempts to individualize programs of studies, initiation of subject-matter or "content" studies at progressively earlier levels (primary, intermediate, and secondary), and supporting federal grants. Special problems dealt with in the recent literature of adolescence include cognitive development, the youth subculture, adolescence in other cultures, cultural deprivation, and the dropout. All have implications for the educational program.

Vocational Education

A major new development in vocational education is in the area occupational center, which permits the pupil to receive occupational training while maintaining membership in his home high school.

The "platform" of vocational education for the present and future includes certain factors or conditions:

1. Consideration of social and economic needs and mores.
2. Recognition of the crucial importance of technology.
3. Conceptual understanding of vocational education in the educative process.
4. Reality of the actual program in the secondary schools.
5. Emphasis upon vocational goals.
6. Extensive development in post-high school institutions.
7. Federal encouragement and review.
8. An effective administrative structure.
9. Interests "outside" public education.

10. Critical analysis and evaluation.

Adult Education

High in the priority of research and future development in the field of adult education are the following questions:

1. By what means can the educational, technical, scientific, and cultural illiterate be educated for economic and social self-sufficiency?

2. What are the most appropriate conditions for adult learning? What are the personal (internal) and social (external) factors that lead to changed behavior in adults?

3. Under what conditions can a teacher be most effective in motivating and stimulating adults to accept change? What communication variables relate to acceptance of change?

4. In what ways can the existing socioeconomic and cultural information be used effectively in planning and conducting programs of continued learning?

5. What are the factors of sociocultural change that most influence learning? In what areas of human concern are educator-induced social actions useful? In what ways can positive action be stimulated? What is the nature of community dynamics; how can it be harnessed to influence learning?

6. Who are the participants in adult education? What has been the quality and quantity of participation in the past? What is it likely to be in the future?

7. What resources within the instructional group can be used to maximize the achievement of individual and group objectives?

8. What are effective means of achieving competence in one's life that are satisfactory to family, social group, community, vocation, and one's role as an individual?

Aging is an important aspect of adult education. In human society at large, and in scholarly and professional fields as well, we have the major problem of social usefulness, in relation to early creativity and long continued productivity. Investigations report the age decade of the Thirties as a high point in the creative productions of scholars and scientists. Group means, however, tell us nothing about individual performance; each of one investigator's contributions may have far more merit than the best works of certain other individuals. Since a fruitful professional or scholarly life, or a full life more generally, includes far more than professional, occupational, or public achievement, there is no good reason for anyone at any age level to feel that his usefulness is at an end. Probably the all-pervading question in aging and in geriatrics is whether one can hope to approximate Robert Browning's wishful insight:

> Grow old along with me!
> The best is yet to be,
> The last of life, for which the first was made.

Higher Education

The community or "people's college" now is more than a continuation of secondary education, with a major emphasis on terminal and vocational education. During the past few years the community college has been widely studied (and established) in terms of philosophy and objectives, present and future role in the community, financial support, and relationships to elementary-secondary education and to the university program.

The urgent problems of higher education are well represented in the literature of recent years:

1. The apparently unlimited expectations of the people for higher education, as represented in the great enrollment increases.

2. Lag in adequate facilities.

3. Shortage of college and university teachers, including community-college personnel.

4. Limited knowledge concerning the nature and function of higher learning.

5. The rapid growth or "explosion" of knowledge, together with increasing demands on higher education.

6. The culture-wide disturbance in value systems, especially among youth.

7. Continuing financial pressures.

8. Threats to freedom, particularly from the extreme right and left.

It has been urged that major qualitative changes are imperative in planning for the future of higher education, especially in improvement of the quality of human relationships in the undergraduate college, including far better integration of the cognitive and noncognitive dimensions of human growth and development:[1]

1. Extensive experimentation in modification of teacher-student relationships and living conditions on campus.

2. Research on the educational applications of developmental psychology and on the means for providing a liberal education for students whose academic aptitude is low as measured by conventional instruments.

---

[1]Joseph F. Kauffman *et al.*, *The Student in Higher Education*. New Haven, Conn.: Hazen Foundation, 1968. vii + 66 pp.

3. Emphasis on the freshman year as an orientation to learning rather than as a first year of sequential academic instruction, reasonable class size, and reduction of competition for marks.

4. A faculty of men and women whose primary concern is facilitation of the learning experiences of students, and freedom for the undergraduate college to operate independent of the professional academic guilds or graduate departments.

5. Appropriate student participation in educational policy making, democratization of rule making and enforcement on campus, and improvement of housing and eating facilities in the interest of a higher quality of human relationships.

6. Serious consideration of how "volunteer" service can be closely integrated with the educational experience, and more flexible arrangements for spreading the required time in college, especially in dealing with the tyranny of fixed prerequisites and established sequences of courses.

Section IV (R)
INDIVIDUAL DIFFERENCES

No two children are exactly alike; yet all have similar needs and motivations, and learn in about the same ways. There are common stages of development through which all children pass, although at different rates. Children are not alike even in the same family. Some are impulsive; others are more composed and less assertive. Some are independent and aggressive; others are easily guided. Some have much vitality and vigor; others have less stamina.

Children develop at different rates physically, mentally, socially, and emotionally. Chronological age alone is an inadequate measure of what a child can and should do. One child may be the same age as another but several inches taller and have stronger muscles. One may be more friendly and work more easily with classmates. One may learn from the printed page more readily than another but have less ability along some other lines. In all age groups, some children are ahead of others in their physical, mental, social, or emotional development. The faster-maturing child may easily go ahead of his age group, but the child maturing more slowly may be pressed too hard to keep up with his age group.

Although the nature of society and the resulting educational needs of citizenship determine what should be taught, the nature of children (the ways in which they learn, and their individual differences) determines how it can be taught, to what extent it can be taught, and when it can be best taught. The life needs of children in our society determine what should be taught and the nature of children determines method.

ADAPTING TO INDIVIDUAL DIFFERENCES

Two methods of adapting the curriculum to individual differences are widely used in the first eight grades: (1) the traditional method of varying the rates at which pupils progress through the grades, and (2) the more recently developed practice of varying the depth and scope of essential topics in the curriculum. Both procedures are used in varying degrees concurrently by most school systems.

These two methods are continued in grades nine through twelve, where a third method is added. Here all pupils do not study the same subjects. The topics and subjects themselves vary with the individual

*capacities and needs of pupils. Specialized courses for specific purposes
are added. In these grades, the curriculum includes more than necessary
general education. An extensive program of extracurricular activities,
and sometimes related work experience out of school, further adapt the
curriculum to individual differences.*

Adaptation of Topics

*The adaptation of essential topics to the individual differences of
pupils is very important and should perhaps be illustrated. Note the
adaptation of a topic in arithmetic—decimal fractions—to the individual
differences of pupils. All our citizens should master two-place decimals.
Every citizen should be able to use his money efficiently, and our money
system involves two-place decimals. The financial page of a newspaper
uses two-place decimals. Rainfall is expressed in hundredths of an inch.
Simple percentage is a two-place decimal. Two-place decimals are so
widely used in everyday life that all citizens need a good working mastery of them. Even the slower pupils, who cannot learn more, should
master two-place decimals thoroughly.*

*Attempts to teach pupils more than they can understand leaves them
confused and helpless. It is better to teach the slower pupils a narrow
scope and depth of essential topics thoroughly than to attempt more
and merely confuse them. It is better to know a little well than to mis-
understand a lot. Average pupils can and should achieve deeper understandings and wider skills. Each pupil, regardless of his ability, should
achieve in the essential topics in every subject to the limit of his individual capacity.*

*Exceptionally gifted pupils should learn not only decimal fractions,
but also the basic underlying principles of decimal notation. They
should see that decimal notation, with place value, required the inven-
tion of zero, which is needed to hold the place when nothing is there.
They should see why we could not have had modern science and technology with the Roman number system. The practical Romans saw no
need for zero, because they thought that if one had nothing he would
not need a figure to represent it. We owe a great debt to the Arabs,
who brought decimal notation to the Western world. (The Indians in
Central America also had zero and represented it by the picture of an
empty clam shell.)*

*The gifted pupils should see that we have decimal notation because
we have ten fingers and that we would have had a better number system
if we had twelve fingers. A billion would then be a number more easily
comprehended, and more decimal fractions would come out even be-*

cause twelve is evenly divisable by more numbers than is ten. Very superior pupils might solve some problems in other number systems.

Superior pupils should see that in the warm countries the people had inefficient number systems based on 20 because they counted around both hands and both feet. Thus the Bible reckons in "scores." On the contrary, the Eskimo tribes in their cold lands have a number system based on five, the fingers of only one hand. The peasants of northern Russia have a number system based on two, and the Univac machine operates on a two-place number system.

The gifted pupils should delve into the history, philosophy, science, and art of every essential topic in the curriculum to the limit of their capacities to achieve. This is good not only for them, but for the other pupils as well. Their supplementary reports and discussions stimulate the slower pupils. All topics in the curriculum lend themselves easily to such enrichment, provided the class has suitable materials. Each pupil, regardless of his ability, should begin each day where he is and take what is for him his own next step, and be so taught that he gets maximum satisfaction and joy out of his educational achievement.

Special Classes

City school systems usually make special provision for those pupils who, because of physical, mental, emotional, or social handicaps, cannot be taught efficiently in classes with normal children. This provision usually includes specially equipped classrooms or separate schools, and teachers with special training.

Further individualization is provided through such procedures as: pre-primary and reading readiness classes for pupils entering elementary schools with inadequate maturity for beginning reading; instructional materials carefully adapted to the varying needs, interests, and reading levels of pupils; and systematically planned contacts with parents to develop cooperative programs of pupil adjustment. The schools provide a planned curriculum adapted to the individual differences and needs of pupils.

CLASSIFICATION OF PUPILS

The classification of pupils is a major responsibility of school administration. Responsibility for the organization of pupils into classes, including promotion policy, is usually vested by the board of education in the superintendent, who in turn delegates authority to school principals and teachers. The major question in each case is, "Where should this pupil be placed so that he can best learn those things that he needs most to learn?" This is to say, "In what class and under what teacher can he best be taught?"

In most school systems there are definite periods when classes are re-organized, usually at the end of the school year. However, school systems usually keep the organization somewhat flexible, with the reassignment of a few pupils throughout the year as instructional needs require. In addition to the problem of whether a pupil can work well with a particular class, there are sometimes personality conflicts that can be resolved by transferring a pupil to another class.

The Spread of Classes

Because of their differences in ability, pupils working at full potential progress at widely varying rates. With good teaching, any class continues to spread until the range of the class in instructional needs is finally so wide that the pupils cannot be effectively taught by group procedures. A class that has a small spread at the beginning of the school year will have a much larger spread by the end of the term. The better the pupils are taught, the faster and wider the class spreads, until by the end of the school year the class spread is usually so wide that the extreme pupils should be reassigned to other classes to reduce the spread.

This periodic reexamination and reduction of the spread in the instructional needs of classes result in the "promotion" and "retardation" of pupils. It is impossible, of course, to eliminate entirely the spread in classes. The most that can be done is to reduce the spread in order to make a class as teachable as possible.

Group Instruction Necessary

In the program of universal education which the American public school system provides, pupils are taught primarily by group instruction. Under group instruction, the pupils learn not only from their teacher but also from each other and from the activities of the class as a whole. Some concepts, such as democracy and brotherhood, and most attitudes, such as loyalty, can be best developed by group instruction. Some outcomes, such as the skills in arithmetic and handwriting, can be better achieved by individual instruction. But group techniques are also helpful with these skills, when wholesome competition or group projects are employed to motivate achievement.

Good class instruction carries over into the out-of-class life of the pupils. When well taught, pupils work independently of the teacher part of the time. The good teacher tries to make every pupil eventually his own best teacher. In their independent work, the pupils work more as *individuals. It is the individual who learns, and the instruction is finally individualized. With suitable materials, the independent work can be individualized to any extent desirable.*

Most schools emphasize both group instruction and individual work. The two are interrelated and interdependent. Classes should be organized, as far as possible, to permit class or group instruction whenever the teacher finds it more effective and economical. Good teachers often divide any class temporarily into subgroups and committees, but if a teacher is forced by the nature of the class to divide the class into too many groups or to abandon group instruction and resort to individual instruction much of the time, the teacher is severely handicapped. Any teacher with a normal-sized class must make much use of group instruction.

If pupils are classified on the assumption that they are to be taught primarily by individual instruction, the teacher should have not more than five or six pupils. It is much more difficult to teach six pupils spread through six grades (one each in grades one, two, three, four, five, and six) than to teach 30 pupils who are similar enough in instructional needs that they can be taught together chiefly by group methods and with the same instructional materials.

The big problem of the old one-room school was the spread of its pupils. In recent years, most one-teacher rural schools have been closed and the pupils transported to larger centers, not because the one-room schools were too large but chiefly because their spread was too great. After closing these schools to organize teachable classes, we should not now re-create the problems of the one-room rural school in consolidated and city school classrooms.

Both group and individual instruction requires the use of suitable materials. Teachers must have the materials and other facilities with which the pupils can be effectively taught both in groups and as individuals.

Teachability of Classes

Three factors determine the teachability of a class: the size of the class; the spread in its instructional needs; and the supply of suitable materials. The class may be too large, the spread of its instructional need may be too wide, the instructional materials may be inadequate, or there may be some combination of these three factors that limits the quality of instruction.

Two of these factors are often confused. Teachers often react adversely to the size of classes when the real difficulty is the spread of the classes.

When he has a few pupils who cannot be taught with the class, a teacher is inclined to assume that they would be eliminated if the class size were reduced, but when the class size is reduced without reduction in class spread, the problem remains.

The handicap of class size is apparent, as is the importance of instructional materials. They are limiting factors worthy of careful attention, but the spread of classes is the only one of the factors controlled by the classification of pupils, and is, therefore, our chief concern in this discussion.

Grouping in the Primary Grades

Thirty pupils, six years old, who are mature enough at the opening of school for beginning reading, can be successfully taught by one teacher in the same room for one school year, because during the year it is usually not necessary to divide the class into more than three groups for reading instruction. The spread of the class has become too wide when the pupils must be divided into more than three groups of reading.

Two 20-minute periods of reading instruction daily (accompanied by supplementary reading activities) are necessary in grades one and two for normal pupils to make satisfactory progress in reading. With three groups, this means ($2 \times 3 \times 20 = 120$) two hours each day for the teacher. With more than three groups, her reading time is increased and the teacher must either neglect reading or omit other essentials of a good program. To omit half of the necessary reading instruction and expect the pupils to make normal progress would be equivalent to reducing the food of an infant by one-half and expecting it to develop a robust and healthy body. When a teacher in grade one or two must organize more than three reading groups, the spread of the class should be reduced by an interchange of a few pupils from the top and/or bottom of the class with some other classes.

In the primary grades, the major objective is teaching pupils to read. In all reading instruction, any group to be taught together should be similar enough in their reading levels so that they can be taught effectively with the same materials. Instruction in reading should have priority in the primary grades and in the programs of all pupils in other grades who cannot use reading profitably in the study of other subjects. Reading is an important factor in grouping pupils on all grade levels.

Steps or Levels Versus Grades

Attempts have been made in some school systems to solve the classification problem in the primary grades by abolishing "grades" and sub-

stituting several "steps" or "levels" for each grade. But when the steps are defined, the new plan is merely a new graded system with more grades, and the plan is usually abandoned. The word "grade" comes from the Latin, gradus, *meaning step. A change from "grades" to "steps" merely substitutes Anglo-Saxon for Latin. Such changes in terminology solve no educational problems. Wherever the plan of "steps" has worked satisfactorily, not more than three "steps" have been assigned to a teacher at any one time. Where more than three levels have been assigned to a teacher, the plan has usually been abandoned. The answer is not steps or levels versus grades, but the number of teachable groups to a teacher.*

Grouping in the Intermediate Grades

In grades four, five, and six, the teacher should be able to work much of the time, if he desires, with the class as a whole. It should not be necessary on account of the spread of the class to divide the class in these groups into more than two groups at any time. With two groups, the teacher can work with each group half of the time. When well taught, pupils in these grades can profitably work independently half of the time, but ordinarily not more.

The third grade may have two or three groups, depending on the educational program. If textbooks and reading materials in the other subjects are introduced in the third grade, and reading instruction is emphasized in these subjects, one 30-minute period of specialized reading instruction daily is sufficient for average pupils to make normal progress. In this case, the grouping in grade three is similar to that in grades four through six. But if the curriculum and materials of grade three follow the plan of grades one and two, the grouping and reading periods should then follow the pattern of grades one and two.

In the intermediate grades, for pupils who have normal reading achievement, the chief objective is basic general elementary education with continued emphasis on reading and the other skill subjects. Pupils are taught both reading and other subjects with equal emphasis. In the other subjects, an instructional group should either be able to read the same materials on the topic under study or be supplied adequately with suitable differentiated materials.

Grouping in the High School

In grades seven through twelve, most of the independent work of the pupils may be in the absence of the teacher. In these grades, with more specialized teaching assignments, the teacher should be able to work with the class as a whole as much as he desires and not be forced by the spread of the class to divide the pupils at any time. This requires a good guidance program and careful attention to the classification of pupils.

As pupils progress in high school, they naturally tend to group with other pupils of similar interests and needs, or with the same vocational plans. This is particularly true in senior high schools where future educational needs, vacational interests, and life-career motives influence the selection of programs and elective subjects. But special attention to classification is necessary in subjects required of all pupils. In high schools, pupils are first classified by their programs and the subjects that make up their programs. Beyond this, the reading level of pupils is an important consideration in all subjects that involve reading.

Significant Factors

How should pupils be classified so they can be most effectively taught? What are the important factors that should determine the grouping of pupils? There are eleven factors to be considered.

1. Pupils who should be taught the same things are grouped together.

2. The members of a group should be able to engage in the same activities.

3. They should be able to use the same materials and facilities.

4. A common minimum level of reading achievement is necessary in most school subjects.

5. Similar general achievement in other subjects is helpful.

6. In some cases physical maturity is important.

7. Sometimes social maturity is a factor.

8. Occasionally emotional maturity is a factor.

9. Mental age limits what a pupil can be taught.

10. The intelligence quotient (unimportant in itself) influences other factors.

11. Chronological age, like the intelligence quotient, has no significance except its influence on other factors.

Pupils should be classified according to the most desirable combination of all significant factors. The use of any one factor alone does not work well. When pupils are grouped homogeneously by a single factor, classes usually spread too widely on other factors.

Combining Significant Factors

Perhaps these factors should be combined into simpler working criteria for the classification, assignment, and grouping of pupils. What is to be taught, instructional activities, and the ability to use materials (factors

1, 2, and 3) may be combined under the heading "desired program." Physical, social, and emotional maturity and mental age (factors 6, 7, 8, and 9) may be combined under "maturity of pupils." The other two significant factors (reading level and general achievement, 4 and 5) might stand alone. The remaining two factors (intelligence quotient and age, 10 and 11) may be disregarded.

The factors to be considered in the classification of pupils may thus be combined roughly into four: program, reading, general achievement, and maturity.

Given the program, the reading level is at first most important, but in the middle grades, general achievement may approach comparable significance. At adolescence, physical maturity takes precedence over other factors in assigning pupils to schools. Children vary widely in the ages at which they become adolescent. Adolescence (physical maturity) is the important factor, not chronological age. The organization of a school system into elementary schools, junior high schools, and senior high schools serves in part to separate preadolescents, early adolescents, and later adolescents. This separation is provided by the 6-3-3 plan of school organization, which is based upon maturity, reading level, and general achievement.

Homogeneous Grouping

A few years ago, many school systems grouped pupils homogeneously by the intelligence quotient, but the use of this plan has declined. A relatively wide spread in I.Q. presents no great difficulty with group methods if other factors are conducive to group procedures. It is what has happened to pupils as a result of the I.Q., not their I.Q. itself, that should be considered. The I.Q. should not arbitrarily determine the class or group to which a pupil is assigned, but should influence how soon he may be reassigned.

The term "homogeneous grouping" is widely misunderstood. All school systems classify pupils homogeneously, and differ only in the emphasis which they place upon the several factors considered in grouping. Placing beginning six-year-old children together is homogeneous grouping by entering age. Placing all seven-year-old children in the second grade, all eight-year-olds in the third grade, all nine-year-olds in the fourth grade, and so on, is homogeneous grouping by age. The no-failure plan, sometimes called "social promotion," is homogeneous grouping by chronological age.

Grouping by age is called the "no-failure plan" because a pupil is "advanced" to the next grade regardless of achievement and other sig-

nificant factors. This produces an excessive spread in the instructional needs of classes. The same size suit of clothes does not fit all ten-year-old boys, and they vary as widely in their instructional needs as in the size of clothes which they wear. All ten-year-old boys should not be put into the same size shoes just because they are the same age. Age has no significance in classifying pupils except in its relationship to other factors.

Normal Progress

Most pupils make normal progress and complete the first eight grades by the time they are fourteen years old. All pupils should normally complete the first eight grades by the time they are sixteen. They should be taught, to the limit of their abilities, the essentials of the common school curriculum before they reach the legal leaving age, which in most states is sixteen. A pupil should not therefore ordinarily "fail" more than twice in the first eight grades. If *(after "failing" twice)* a pupil cannot be satisfactorily taught with his classmates, he should be transferred to an ungraded or remedial class. *School systems usually organize such special classes on two levels, one for younger pupils and one for older pupils.*

Usually the lowest 2 percent of all pupils is organized in special classes for slow learners, for whom an adapted program is provided. This is done not only for the good of these slow pupils but also so that other pupils may be taught more effectively when the very slow pupils are removed from the regular classes. In the same way, some school systems organize mentally gifted pupils in separate classes.

The best classification of pupils and their assignment to teachers are finally a matter of good judgment in the light of the controlling factors. It cannot be reduced to arbitrary rule and administered by a clerk. There can be no formula that relieves the school principal from the responsibility for a high degree of sound judgment as he cooperates with teachers and parents in the proper classification of pupils and their assignments to teachers. It is largely this important phase of school organization that makes the school principal the key to a good educational program.

GOOD TEACHING

Teaching is the process of giving direction to education and speeding up the rate at which learning takes place. The direction of education is determined by what is taught and the rate is determined chiefly by how it is taught. Good teaching is the best use of all available resources to accomplish the desired purposes of the school.

The good teacher understands his pupils, knows the kind of citizens that society requires, and uses efficiently all available educational re-

sources. The good teacher gives desired direction to education and speeds up in maximum degree the rate at which education takes place by using wisely all available means of instruction. Each particular resource is used in the way it can best serve in the instructional program.

The good teacher uses textbooks, supplementary books, encyclopedias, dictionaries, maps, globes, charts, chalkboards, workbooks, films, slides, recordings, current periodicals, museums, historical sites, parks, zoos, factories and business institutions, and all other community resources, using no one particular resource when some other resource or combination of resources would serve the purposes better. Although the good teacher uses many resources and a variety of activities, the basic learning activities in most school subjects are reading and discussion.

To learn from others through reading and discussion, children require a rich background of firsthand personal experience. Suitable provision for necessary conceptual background and learning readiness is an essential element of good teaching. Children must therefore have many opportunities to construct, apply, demonstrate, illustrate, think, express, and appreciate.

Good teaching provides for pupils to acquire and maintain a sense of personal worth and belonging, with a feeling of security and freedom from burdensome fears and anxieties. A child must learn to meet and profit from failure, but continuous and repeated failure often destroys self-confidence, and may breed a spirit of futility. The life of every child should be characterized, on the whole, by a success pattern and a feeling of personal worth and security.

Interest is a large factor in learning. Teachers and parents have responsibility for the interests of children as well as for what they learn. Good teaching begins with the present interests of children and develops new interests that are educationally more significant. Good teaching creates situations that interest children in those things in which they must be interested in order to teach them the things they should be taught. There are no uninteresting things in the universe, although there may be some uninterested pupils.

Good teaching presupposes good teachers. Concern must be expressed over the difficulty of enlisting a sufficiently large number of talented young people to the teaching profession. The schools are handicapped by being in competition with aggressive business and industry. The problem is one of retention, too. The schools endeavor to make teaching situations attractive, but the rewards for teachers must be equivalent to the rewards for comparable talent in other pursuits. The teacher shortage is one of the most serious problems confronting our public schools.

INSTRUCTIONAL MATERIALS

Increasing enrollments and heavy teaching loads place new emphasis on an adequate supply of instructional materials. Good teaching requires and uses a variety of materials. In recent years much improvement has been made in instructional materials and in their effective use. Textbooks, supplementary books, encyclopedias, dictionaries, pamphlets, newspapers, magazines, films, recordings, charts, workbooks, exhibits, radio and television programs, pictures, and many other resources are used in diverse ways. A good textbook serves as the organizing basis of a well-planned course of instruction, but textbooks alone are not sufficient for a satisfactory program. Many other instructional aids are necessary. The quality of instruction is limited by the supply and wise use of appropriate teaching materials. The provision of adequate teaching equipment and instructional materials is an important responsibility of the community.

The careful appraisal and selection of instructional materials are an important function of school administration. Textbooks are usually adopted on the recommendation of carefully selected, well-balanced committees of teachers, supervisors, and administrators who thoroughly examine all available publications. Teacher cooperation is also used in the appraisal and selection of other important instructional materials in general use, but the administration retains the ultimate responsibility for selection.

Some materials are supplied directly to classrooms; some are cataloged and stored in the individual school for distribution within the school; and some are usually stored in a central teaching-aids center and circulated to schools as needed. The central collection usually includes motion picture films and other important materials not in continuous use and too expensive to assign permanently to individual schools, and which can be easily circulated throughout the school system.

Free and inexpensive materials are extensively used, but require careful screening. To illustrate propaganda techniques, the schools may use almost any materials which circulate freely in the community and to which the pupils are exposed in their daily lives, but such materials are used under careful teacher supervision, with due attention to their partisan nature. The point of view, purpose, and standing of the sponsoring organization are noted.

Although partisan materials are used in the analysis of propaganda techniques, every precaution is exercised to guarantee that textbooks and basic references are not only authentic and comprehensive but are also objective and impartial. School systems exercise great care in the ap-

praisal, selection, purchase, distribution, and maintenance of all types of instructional materials and teaching equipment. The high quality and adequate supply of these facilities are second in importance only to the teacher in maintaining acceptable standards of instruction.

HOMEWORK

Most school systems plan for some supplementary homework in the intermediate grades, a little more in the upper grades, and still more (and sometimes work experience) on the high school level, but this is so planned that pupils work successfully, and without direct parental assistance, on projects which are an extension of school work. It is planned so as not to interfere with, but instead to supplement, the desirable home life of children. The good school develops educational momentum that permeates the home lives of pupils so that they live continuously out of school what they are being taught in school.

In general, the skills and other fundamentals are taught in school, and are motivated and maintained, in part, through use at home. The schools teach children to read, and the children then use reading at home to learn many interesting things, and to use their leisure time wisely. The schools teach spelling and letter-writing, and pupils at home write letters to their friends and relatives. The girl learns home economics in school and joins her mother in applying it in the home. The schools teach geography, history, and civics, with due attention to the current scene, and pupils out of school take an active interest in current affairs.

The content subjects require much enrichment in real-life situations. When well taught they extend into out-of-school life on a problem-approach basis which continues the development of the important basic concepts in these fields. The home thus provides opportunities for using what is taught, for learning many practical skills, and for building attitudes and habits which continue education in later life. Thus homework extends, motivates, applies, vitalizes, and enriches the school curriculum.

Education and living are continuous and unbroken. Children learn what they live and then live what they have learned. The educative process operates throughout our waking hours, and, although the schools provide an essential part of our education (without which civilization could not exist), the home is our most important educational institution. It is largely at home and in the community that one acquires his language, his religion, his politics, and most of the deep-seated attitudes that determine his character. The home and the school have their own special educational functions to perform, and neither can take the place of the other. Education is a cooperative enterprise.

REPORTING TO PARENTS

Most school systems keep detailed and systematic records and periodically report to parents the progress of pupils. The type and frequency of reports vary throughout the country; and within a single school system the method of reporting to parents is not usually the same on all grade levels. Primary teachers are usually closer in touch with the parents of their pupils than are high school teachers, and reports to parents of primary pupils are usually somewhat less formal than reports to parents of high school pupils.

Most schools use a five-point marking system in high schools and sometimes a somewhat narrower range of marks in elementary schools, particularly in the primary grades. Reports to parents usually indicate the interest and application of pupils, as well as their educational achievement. But report cards alone are not sufficient to keep the home and school adequately in touch with each other, and such reports are supplemented by appropriate personal conferences as needs require. The closest possible cooperation between home and school, with fullest mutual understanding, is necessary to operate a good educational program that adequately meets the needs of pupils.

Section IV

ADAPTATION TO INDIVIDUAL DIFFERENCES: INSTRUCTIONAL-LEARNING PROCEDURES

Children do differ in many ways, including needs, motivations, expectations, and learning procedures, as well as in mental, physical, emotional, social, racial, and cultural characteristics.

Class Organization and Grouping

The closing of the traditional one-room school (R) may have been due, not so much to the "spread" or range of the teacher's responsibility as to the high cost of low pupil-teacher ratios and limited opportunity to achieve social objectives. The problems of grouping and "spread" among pupils now are less difficult, with the availability of individualized materials and methods of instruction as media of flexibility.

Traditionally, the elementary classroom has been a self-contained unit in which one professional (teacher) has taught a number of pupils (usually five to 35) of a given age for the total school program. During recent years modifications in this practice, developed to improve the quality of instruction, have included variations in class size, teacher specialization, and teacher and pupil mobility. For the same purpose, school leaders have developed cooperative teaching, team teaching, a dual-progress plan, the nongraded school, a continuous progress curriculum, and other variations in grouping and scheduling practices. Whatever the organizational plan adopted, community orientation and communication are essential, as well as understanding, adequate preparation, and confidence on the part of teachers, together with administrative cooperation and flexibility.

It is doubtful that class size as such determines "teachability," as compared with the teacher's ability, although class size may well affect work load, teacher frustration, individual help for pupils, and availability of instructional materials. To condemn large classes in general poses an interesting contradiction, in view of present support of team teaching and large-group instruction.

Nongrading is a departure from the conventional graded system for organizing instruction, on the assumption that the grade-level curriculum, placement, and promotion do not provide adequately for individual differences among pupils. Proponents of ungraded classes would argue that such flexibility now is much more than a matter of terminology (R) or a novelty.

In the dual-progress plan a pupil commonly spends nearly half of the day in language arts and social studies with one specialist-teacher, plus a period in physical education, and during the other half of the same day he proceeds from room to room, class to class, and teacher to teacher for instruction in the nongraded subjects.

Individualized teaching is representative of a type of learning-teaching relationship in which the young person: (1) learns or studies independently; (2) learns through creative or diversified activities or by relating another discipline or subject matter to that which he is studying; (3) learns or studies independently in a class or subgroup of the class as a result of the teacher's individualizing behavior on the pupil's behalf.

Team teaching is a cooperative effort of teachers to provide flexibility in grouping pupils, with part of a child's instruction in a small group of three or four and part in larger groups. Several classrooms may be combined for a teacher to demonstrate an experiment to a large group, while a reading specialist is free to help one or two pupils with problems or difficulties. Some schools have large lecture halls, small conference rooms, and study carrels, while other schools alter cafeterias, gymnasiums, and other space in the interest of team teaching. Clerical aides or auxiliary personnel sometimes relieve team teachers of typing, scheduling, and other routine chores.

Outlined in more detail, grouping practices involve number and size of groups, and type of grouping (achievement and/or ability groups, multi-age grouping, pupil teams, and individual or independent study).

The number of groups in which a child is placed seems to have greatest effect on social-emotional development, attitudes, and interests, probably because pupils come in contact with more children and adults.

The idea of static class size (20-30 pupils) has been challenged by organizational innovations (8-12 for discussion groups and 5-8 for maximizing pupil and teacher interactions), depending on the nature of the activity, the maturity and ability of the children, and the competence of the teacher. Large groups have been defined as any number from 12 to 400, and hundreds of pupils may be grouped together for films, television, dramatic presentations, and other passive activities. The chief advantages of large-group instruction have been in more effective utilization of teacher time, space, and materials, with teachers freed for planning, preparation, and working with individuals or small groups.

The studies of homogeneous grouping during nearly a half century have failed to show consistent statistically or educationally significant differences between the achievement of pupils so placed and children of equal ability in heterogeneous groups. Only when general ability grouping is accompanied by appropriate adaptation of means and materials of instruction is there better achievement in homogeneous classes.[2] Differential regrouping for each subject has been the practice in many team-teaching and nongraded programs, with good results when accompanied by differentiation in content, method, speed, and/or teacher technique.

Mental age, rather than I.Q. (R), is one basis for grouping pupils, although I.Q. does have meaning when working with a group uniform in chronological age or mental age.

The teacher may be freed to provide individual attention where most needed, through use of pupil teams or small groups (two or three children working together, largely independent of the teacher's instruction) and individual or independent study plans, often with the aid of concrete objects, programmed texts and computer-assisted instruction, other multi-media, and such devices as the talking typewriter and closed-circuit and educational TV.

Variations of scheduling practices have been developed—block, core, and modular. Block scheduling may provide cooperative planning time for teachers. Core scheduling at the elementary level usually refers to a social studies-language arts curriculum taught by one teacher to pupils of approximately the same age. The plan is intended to facilitate economical use of materials, and increase teacher specialization and departmentalization. Modular scheduling is an alternative to the static period of 50 minutes, one hour, or other length. Modules of 15, 20, 30, or any number of minutes may be used to meet the needs of pupils, teacher, or special activity, chiefly in secondary schools, and at the same time facilitate administrative organization.

Special Education

The broad area of exceptional children includes the mentally retarded, gifted, speech handicapped, deaf and hard of hearing, learning disorderd and educationally handicapped, emotionally maladjusted, socially disadvantaged, and physically crippled. The literature of recent years relating to exceptional children indicates certain trends:

1. A tendency to relate research to a theoretical frame of reference.

2. An increase in investigations other than status and descriptive studies.

3. Increased use of the team or interdisciplinary approach.

4. More concern for problems of children with multiple handicaps.

5. Further refinement in terminology and in measurement-diagnostic procedures.

[2]Esin Kaya and Others, *Developing a Theory of Educational Practice for the Elementary School.* Norwalk, Conn.: Board of Education, 1967. pp. 19-77.

6. Grouping for instruction based on common educational problems or needs rather than on greater homogeneity achieved through more precise or fixed classifications of exceptionality.

The problems facing the gifted child include certain emotional and motivational difficulties, adjustment of his intellectual interests and skills to the curriculum being offered in the classroom and to systematic instructional procedures, and relationships with other children. The challenge to the teacher of the gifted is formidable indeed, in terms of the wide range of intellectual difference in the class, the absence of adequate information about the children, and extensive knowledge and skill required in a number of curriculum areas. Certainly the teacher of the gifted child will evaluate him on the basis of his own potential (rather than his comparative status in the group) and will encourage development of creativity and originality.

Among the problems involving the retarded child are the large number of dropouts from high school, disappearance of unskilled occupations, and the complexity of occupational and social situations. The classroom teacher may well deal with the educable mentally retarded child by evaluation in accordance with his level of performance as suggested by the pupil's intellectual status (and not by the standards set for the rest of the class), by engagement in a program of learning consonant with healthy social and emotional growth, and by development of realistic attitudes toward school and self.

The investigators and observers who describe and enumerate the characteristics of socially disadvantaged children need to translate this information more fully into meaningful learning experiences. There probably is no typical "socially disadvantaged child," but instead a variety of such children, with widely varying characteristics. The mere fact of a relationship between certain conditions or characteristics and poor school adjustment or underdevelopment does not establish causation or point clearly to a definite course of remediation. The general premise that the common educational handicaps of socially disadvantaged children can be largely remedied through appropriate school experiences is supported by psychological and sociological theory, but much work must be done to develop and evaluate sound educational programs.

Certain favorable school conditions for preventing undesirable behavior, juvenile deliquency, or social deviancy are as follows:

1. To know and accept the delinquent as a person.
2. To locate the predelinquent early.
3. To maintain an impersonal and objective point of view.
4. To take a diagnostic look at causal factors underlying misbehavior.

5. To foster cooperation between school and community agencies, with special services for the delinquent.

6. To differentiate instruction.

7. To use the effective teacher personality as an example of desirable behavior and achievement.

8. To involve the delinquent in his own rehabilitation.

9. To maintain a reasonable school and class size.

During the past few years a considerable body of literature has appeared on guidance of pupils with special characteristics, including the superior or gifted, specialty-oriented students (such as those who enter terminal vocational training programs at the post-secondary school level), and the culturally deprived or disadvantaged. The school counselor during recent years has been viewed increasingly as a member of a pupil personnel team, cooperating closely with the school psychologist, school nurse, and school social worker. More frequent references are now made in the literature to the foundations of guidance, counseling, and personnel services in philosophy, sociology, and psychology.

INSTRUCTION AND LEARNING

Through a quarter of a century the literature on the image of the teacher has changed from that of transmitter of knowledge to diagnostician, guide, and interactive participant in the educative process, in the interest of the pupil's objectives of cognitive growth, social effectiveness, self-direction, and favorable attitude development. This concept of the teacher and instruction is more significant than the particular teaching method employed (such as lecture, discussion, project, recitation, demonstration, or critical thinking). In general, when teachers select goals in keeping with the needs of pupils, state such goals clearly in terms of pupil outcomes, and devise appropriate evaluative techniques, then a climate conducive to learning is provided.

After a century of essentially standard design and specifications, even the architecture of many school buildings has changed from standards of indestructibility and cheapness to the criteria of function, beauty, comfort, and adaptability to living and learning.

Development of Creative Behavior

Teachers may well select or adapt certain principles and procedures in facilitating the development of creative behavior among pupils:

1. Emphasize purpose and communication in creative writing.

2. Provide experiences that make children more sensitive to environmental stimuli.

3. Develop a constructive rather than a hypercritical attitude toward informational and learning materials.

4. Avoid situations or illustrations that may "freeze" or unduly shape the creative thinking of pupils.

5. Avoid too frequent or too formal evaluation.

6. Make it clear that originality is encouraged and will be appropriately rewarded.

Development of Desirable Intergroup Relations

Understanding and development of desirable intergroup relations, as an important instructional objective, are fostered through certain school practices:

1. Avoiding invidious comparisons between groups.

2. Recognizing that changes in attitudes are also changes in feelings.

3. Helping individuals change their attitudes toward others through specific kinds of direct experience (including contacts with minority-group individuals of high achievement) and helping children see the meaning of such experiences.

4. Recognizing the difference between surface behavior and under-the-surface feelings.

5. Helping children acquire empathy with others.

6. Using even conflict situations to further understanding of intergroup relations.

Development of Mental Health and Emotional Maturity

As an instructional objective, sound mental health includes objective judgment, initiative or self-direction (autonomy), emotional maturity, self-realizing drive, self-acceptance, and respect for others. The school is a great potential source for growth and development of children in a number of areas related to mental health and emotional maturity:

1. The teacher, as compared with many parents, is in a better position to help the child think in an organized, objective manner.

2. For many children the school provides the only planned, continuous experience in learning, where they can determine and work toward goals.

3. The school is in a favorable position to teach all the children the basic facts and principles of human behavior.

4. The teacher, by example, may encourage self-appraisal and self-understanding, as well as an attitude of wanting to understand other people.

The teacher's understanding and acceptance of himself are important in helping the pupil know himself and in developing a healthy attitude of self-acceptance on the part of the child.

In facilitating instruction, the teacher can improve his control of pupil behavior through attention to his own mental health and emotional stability, a repertoire of techniques for dealing with individual differences, extensive information about class leaders, clarity and firmness in control techniques, focus on learning, expertness in his field of instruction, interest in teaching, and emphasis on reward rather than punishment.

Use of Auxiliary Personnel or Aides

In modern terminology, "auxiliary school personnel" is generally preferred over "teacher aides" or "paraprofessionals." Use of such auxiliary personnel permits the professional teacher to do a better job of teaching, especially in individualizing instruction, small-group work, and team teaching. Auxiliary "aides" may perform a variety of helpful services: clerical duties such as preparing report cards, typing, and mimeographing; library assistance in processing books and in handling circulating and reference works; housekeeping in relation to ventilation and lights, cleanup after art and laboratory classes, preparation of displays, and help with young children's clothing; supervision of halls, lunchrooms, and playgrounds; instructional assistance to teachers in record keeping, laboratories, and audio-visual materials and equipment; and establishing favorable relationships with parents and other citizens of the school community. The increasing use of auxiliary personnel is not intended as a cheaper way to staff the classroom or to render the professional teacher more remote from the children, but to give the teacher time and opportunity for increased insight as he studies the problems and lives of individual pupils.[3]

The experience derived from utilization of auxiliary personnel presents certain common problems of developing effective interaction among professionals, auxiliaries, pupils, and parents in a community-centered school.[4]

1. Effective recruitment and selection procedures for auxiliary personnel, as well as brief preservice programs and vocational counseling.

2. Team training for all staff members, and application of the team approach to both the school as a whole and to the classroom; in effect, "teams within a team."

[3]National Commission on Teacher Education and Professional Standards, *Auxiliary School Personnel*. Washington: N.E.A., 1967. 20 pp.
[4]Garda W. Bowman and Gordon F. Klopf, *New Careers and Roles in the American School: A Study of Auxiliary Personnel in Education*. New York: Bank Street College of Education, for the Office of Economic Opportunity, 1967. ii + 201 pp.

3. Involvement of selected parents as auxiliaries, establishment of school-community advisory boards, and case-by-case analysis of each school situation with appropriate counseling.

4. Assurance of continued funding and priority in the school budget, close cooperation between the schools and collegiate institutions, appropriate in-service programs of training for all school personnel, and additional administrative and supervisory staff for servicing auxiliary personnel.

Multi-Media and Programmed Instruction

During recent years great progress has been made in the development of multi-media means and experiences as major aids to effective instruction, assisted substantially by the merger of business and publishing organizations for the production of printed materials and the "hardware" of instruction. A multi-media learning-teaching situation is one in which learners utilize means, experiences, and processes other than a common textbook and listening, and teachers instruct through other than a common textbook and lecture. Examples of multi-media means are use of more than one of the following: realia, TV, audio-video tape, motion pictures, loop film, recordings, radio, still pictures, maps, diagrams, charts, or several books or periodicals. Examples of multi-experiences are real experiences, including conversation, discussion, introductions, telephoning, interviewing, reporting, asking or answering questions, and writing; contrived experiences using models, mock-ups, objects, and specimens; dramatized experiences such as reenacting, role playing, acting or watching dramatized experiences, demonstration and experimentation such as doing or watching; and field trips.

Certain directions of growth in programmed instruction as an area of important aids to teaching and learning include:

1. A systems approach.
2. Instructional research.
3. Psychological emphasis and behavioral analysis.
4. Behavioral studies of curriculum design.
5. Empirical determination of curricular components.
6. Production and use of instructional materials and environments.
7. Provision for self-instruction.
8. Group-paced programmed instruction.
9. Learning materials and media for the learner.
10. The classroom teacher's role in relation to programmed materials.
11. New ways of evaluating learning and instruction.
12. Increased importance of machines, especially computers.

13. Curriculum and instructional decisions outside the local school.

14. Changes in teacher education.

15. Natural lines of development in technology and unnatural retardation of programming.

Research in Development and Learning

By the late 1960's research in development and learning has indicated increased interest and activity in a number of areas related to instruction:[5]

1. Patterns of mother-child interactions and other aspects of the home situations relating to cognitive development and involving social class differences.

2. Recognition of the various levels of learning as differing in complexity but sharing a great deal of commonality.

3. Social behavior such as cooperation, responsibility, and altruism.

4. Complex relationships among variables significant in the learning process—intelligence level, sex, age, anxiety level, task difficulty, type of instructions, reinforcement utilized, social role of persons present in the learning situation, and nature of the learning task.

5. The cognitive processes in motor-skill learning, particularly in relation to information feedback, reaction time, tracking, and mental practice.

6. Perceptual learning in relation to sensory factors (in contrast to earlier emphasis on operant conditioning); for example, perceptual factors related to the acquisition of reading skill.

7. Computer technology for teaching and research on instruction.

It is now realized that in instructional research we must analyze much smaller units than large complex procedures such as the lecture method, discussion method, or class size.[6] "It may well be that the mean score on a ten-item test of comprehension, adjusted for student ability and content relevance of the lecture, is still too large and complex a dependent variable."

Homework and Reporting To Parents

If it is granted that traditional or routine homework (or busywork) has very limited value, especially in such areas as the social studies, there still remain with us important questions concerning the planning of productive homework. What educational purpose does homework serve? What effect does a particular kind of homework have on pupils of widely

---

[5]R.M.W. Travers *et al.*, "Growth, Development, and Learning." *Review of Educational Research* 37:471-642; December, 1967.

[6]N. L. Gage, "An Analytical Approach to Research on Instructional Methods." *Phi Delta Kappan* 49:601-606; June, 1968.

varying interests, abilities, and achievements? In what other ways might pupils profitably spend their time? Could the desired objectives be achieved by guided study during a better planned and organized school day? Can homework be an extension of the increasing time for independent study in school (for example, flexible scheduling as in library work, laboratory work as in science, a foreign language, or typing)?

Certainly reporting to parents must be considered in terms of its effect on the development and self-image of pupils; for example, competitive marking systems may be self-defeating in the attainment of important educational objectives. To improve reports of pupil progress and development, educators are now placing increased emphasis on conferences between parents, teachers, and counselors.

Section V (R)

ADMINISTRATION

In the American tradition, the public schools belong to the people and are responsive to the will of the community they serve. What they can be, and do, is limited by what the people are willing for them to be and do. What is taught, and even how it is taught, is by consent of the people. Our people are entitled to have the kind of schools they want.

This means that schools are not static. We live in a period of relatively rapid change. Life becomes ever more complex. The frontiers of life and action are no longer physical. Instead, they are political, social, and economic in nature, and worldwide in scope. Although the schools do not take sides on controversial issues or advocate changes in the social order, they must adjust and adapt to change, and endeavor to interpret change dispassionately and objectively. This requires educational leadership with vision that interprets a growing and improving educational program, democratically developed and efficiently administered.

Schools are usually organized and operated under a legally constituted board of education, representing the community and acting for the community in all matters pertaining to the policies of the schools. In good educational administration, the following principles are well established:

1. The people provide a nonpartisan, public-spirited board of education to govern the operation of their schools.

2. The chief functions of the board of education are: (a) legislative, the adoption of policy; (b) the review and evaluation of results; and (c) the interpretation of the program and its needs to the community.

3. The executive function of the board of education is discharged through a competent superintendent of schools and an adequate staff of professional assistants held responsible for the efficient administration of the schools.

4. The review and interpretive functions are discharged by the board of education, the superintendent of schools, and the professional staff, in accordance with policies established by the board of education.

To best achieve their purposes, the schools operate under favorable conditions of widespread community understanding, cooperation, and support. Education is a responsibility which many agencies share. A successful program requires that all agencies achieve their educational purposes in maximum degree.

Section V

ADMINISTRATION, LEADERSHIP, AND THE TEACHER

During recent years research in educational organization and administration has been much less concerned with "administrative theory" and what "the leader" is or does (as an explanation of important events) than with analysis of administrative procedures, instructional approaches, schools, and fiscal structures as systems or system components. The literature now includes teachers as prime interactors with the administrator, the organization as his context or even as the major determinant of what occurs, allocative strategies for human and material resources, and the wide-ranging politico-economic framework of the schools and education. During the earlier part of the present decade, in addition to descriptive information, the literature of administration reflected especially the influence of concepts from the social and behavioral sciences, including sociology, psychology, history, government, economics, politics, and philosophy.

Through the past years of research on administrative practice, personal traits and qualities have been investigated repeatedly, but with limited results in useful data, especially with respect to leadership cause-effect relationships. The studies of administrative behavior may be classified according to traits and personal characteristics; cultural and background knowledge and experience; and administrative style and organizational climate (such as democratic, authoritarian, paternal, or laissez faire).

The great problems of our society cut across professional and scientific specialties. We need leaders, including school administrators, who can see these problems in broad perspective, but we must face the fact that most of our intellectually gifted young people go directly from college to graduate or professional school, thus becoming indoctrinated in a limited set of attitudes and values appropriate for scholars, scientists, and professional men. The worthy achievements of specialization leave little time for developing the "moral" leadership (that is, the nourishing of values appropriate to our time) required of our university presidents, senators, corporation presidents, newspaper editors, school superintendents, and governors.[7]

One difficulty affecting both administrative leadership and innovation is that research has been given relatively low priority in schools

---

[7]John W. Gardner, "The Need for Leaders." *Science* 151:283; January 21, 1966.

of education, as compared with professional field service and instruction. Thus both the recruiting of research staff members and the training of research specialists have been handicapped. Coordinators of research or "managerial scholars" are needed in schools of education (and in federal agencies), to devote their time to intellectual leadership in the interest of gathering evidence and developing innovations in education, with specialized preparation, adequate financial support and staffing, and appropriate faculty rank and tenure. This educational leadership (whether located in universities, school systems, or state and federal agencies) should temper the notion that "educational change for tomorrow" is the only or chief goal of leadership, and should give at least equal attention to the complexities of teaching and learning in our schools today, as well as to administration, in the interest of identifying major principles and long-range policies.[8]

In the research of recent years teacher variables have been related less frequently to pupil outcomes than to other teacher variables. No administrator variable has been directly related to pupil outcomes. Research is concentrated on relating administrator variables to other administrator variables. Effect of pupil variables on educational practice has not been studied (with the exception of a correlation between the intellectual functioning of children and the teacher's evaluative practices). No studies have been reported concerning the effect of curricula on teachers, administrators, and school organization. Should not pupil characteristics and the nature of the curriculum partially determine school organization and the means and methods of instruction, as well as effect some changes in teachers and administrators? One estimate is that pupil variables present on entering school account for 85 percent of the variance in pupil outcomes after attending school, leaving only 15 percent attributable to what took place in school.

The problem of teacher supply and demand should be examined in the context of the social, philosophical, and political aspirations of our society. We need much fuller information in a number of areas:

1. Conditions that influence teacher-education graduates not to enter the profession.

2. Factors that influence prospective teachers in the choice of location for assignment.

3. Characteristics that are significant predictors of success and persistence in different subject areas and grade levels.

---

[8]Sam D. Sieber and Paul F. Lazarsfeld, *The Organization of Educational Research in the United States.* Cooperative Research Project No. 1,974. New York: Columbia University, 1966. xxii + 364 pp.

4. Influence on teacher supply and demand of various staff utilization plans, use of auxiliary personnel, and of curricular innovations.

5. Extent and effect of the misassignment of teachers.

Other urgent problems of teacher status involve tensions between faculty and administration in terms of the theory of "power equalization," relation between salaries (and fringe benefits) and teacher supply, economic and tenure status of teachers belonging to minority groups, and teacher collective action or negotiations.

Certain trends in state certification requirements for teachers are promising:

1. Efforts to refine the structure and processes of NCATE (National Council for the Accreditation of Teacher Education).

2. The steady decrease in the number of separately named certificates issued by the states.

3. The strengthening of the processes of state accreditation (or approval) of teacher-education programs.

4. The emergence of state professional practices acts.

5. The drive for workable procedures toward nationwide reciprocity in teacher certification.

6. The granting of greater autonomy to institutions in developing teacher-education programs.

7. Greater use of national examinations in teacher-education programs, in certification after independent study, and in measurement of prerequisites to certification.

Section VI (R)

MORAL AND SPIRITUAL VALUES

The public schools seek to identify the moral values in the curriculum, focus attention upon them, and teach them effectively. The schools include in the established school subjects the role of religion in the development of civilization, in present-day world affairs, and in American life. The public schools maintain, in all ways and at all times, a climate friendly to religion, but religious indoctrination and the teaching of religion as such are left entirely to the home and the church.

Values Permeate the Program

Moral and spiritual values are essential elements of the public school program. They are present in the various school subjects and extracurricular activities, and are exemplified in the administration of the school. They permeate all phases of the curriculum. These values are not usually treated separately, but are integrated throughout all instructional activities. Their identification is an important step in curriculum development.

The social studies deal continuously with our basic values. Literature emphasizes human values and character delineation. The classics portray the struggle between good and evil. Science and mathematics exalt truth and intellectual honesty. Music and art express the aspirations of the ages. Industrial arts challenge creative abilities. Home economics is concerned with better living. Health and physical education promote good sportsmanship and better human relations. Children learn to live the good life by living it and then continue to live what they have learned.

Inculcating Values

It is mainly through the skill and example of the teacher that moral and spiritual values are most effectively implemented in the school program. Good teaching, with its many examples of integrity and fair dealing, leads pupils to accept and practice these values. The schools provide maximum freedom of choice consistent with acceptable standards of conduct. Honesty is not taught by removing all opportunity to be dishonest; moral responsibility assumes some possibility of choice. By providing realistic opportunities for self-realization, the schools help pupils develop those high moral standards and positive personal convictions by which they strive to live the good life.

The big problem of character education is the motivation of right conduct. *Knowledge of right by itself does not always impel the individual to do right. Memorizing the Ten Commandments does not prevent a person from violating any of them. One does right intentionally only when he wants to do right. One should not only know what is right; he should also want to do what is right. It is easy to teach what is right, but difficult to teach the desires (attitudes and ideals) that motivate right conduct. Deep personal conviction and firm devotion to the true, the beautiful, and the good are necessary to maintain firm habits of good conduct.*

Our Religious Heritage

"We are a religious people whose institutions presuppose a supreme being." The conduct of most Americans is, in varying degrees, religiously motivated. Belief in God brings divine sanction to morality. Moral values, when accepted as the will of God, become spiritual values. Our government was founded on a belief in God. Our money and our national anthem assert that "In God We Trust." Allegiance is pledged to our nation "under God." Most Americans approach the basic values of life through the fatherhood of God and the brotherhood of man. More than 95 per cent of the American people express a belief in God. The public schools reflect this belief. Most children enter school with a firm belief in God.

Religious freedom is also basic in the American way. "Congress shall make no law respecting an establishment of religion, or prohibiting the free exercise thereof. . . ." Our government has no control, supervision, or jurisdiction over religion, but the separation of church and state does not imply that the state is indifferent to religion, nor that the church is indifferent to civic interest. It means that the choice of one's religion is a personal freedom reserved to the individual.

Religion in the Program

The teaching of religion is a responsibility of the home and the church. The public schools support and endeavor to strengthen the home in discharging this important responsibility, but following the example of our government, the public schools, though friendly to religion, are nonsectarian and strictly impartial towards all religions. The schools respect the religion of each child and his belief or disbelief in God as taught by the home. They also teach each child to respect the religious beliefs of others. In individual cases of counseling and discipline, the public schools, in their discretion, may invoke the sanctions accepted by the home.

The public schools deal reverently with references to God as they come up from day to day, but the schools are careful not to infringe upon the right of the home to define, explain, and interpret God. The public schools cannot ignore God. An attempt to ignore God in the school program would be an attempt to deny God. The public schools are not godless. They acknowledge and accept God, but they do not teach God because to teach God is to define and interpret God, and this becomes sectarian. Religion is always a particular religion in the life of an individual. One can no more teach religion without teaching "a religion" than he can teach language to an infant without teaching a specific language. The public schools may not inculcate a religious creed or dogma, nor practice sectarian religious rites. They should not develop separate instructional units on religion divorced from the remainder of the curriculum nor should they ordinarily set aside a separate time in the school day for teaching about religion.

Religion in General Education

Religious orientation, however, is an essential element of general education, and is therefore included in the public school program. The study of music is incomplete without some consideration of church music. The religious motive is prominent in architecture, sculpture, and painting. The religious element has run through the development of literature and the theater in an unbroken thread. Many great wars throughout history have involved some religious issue. Discussion of present-day world affairs, including such countries as Israel, Egypt, and Pakistan, is incomplete without the religious element. The religious factor cannot be ignored in such topics as the Crusades and the Reformation.

Perhaps the interrelation of school subjects should be noted more fully. No school subject can be taught entirely separate from others. For example, note the composition of the social studies. To take mathematics out of the social studies is to remove the calendar, the time sequence, and quantitative data from history and geography. The elimination of science would prevent an explanation of modern technology and our industrial civilization. If music and art were eliminated, we could not fully explain the culture of any people. If the language arts were eliminated, we could neither read nor discuss geography, history, and civics. Although, at any one time, a teacher is usually teaching some one school subject, he must frequently include something from other subjects.

In a similar way, religion permeates most school subjects. Religion may be regarded both as a subject and as a part of other subjects. As a separate subject, religion becomes sectarian and is taught by the home and the church, not by the public schools; but, to the extent that religious orientation is necessary to understand other subjects fully, it is an essential element of general education. A nonsectarian treatment of religion is therefore included in the public-school program wherever it is needed to clarify an instructional objective. To eliminate religion from the school program entirely is to eliminate general education.

Special Days

The public schools observe special days in accordance with this policy. There is almost no limit to the use of Thanksgiving in the schools. But special days with sectarian significance, such as Christmas, Easter, and Yom Kippur, require more careful treatment. The schools take appropriate note of special days widely observed in the community, and much, for example, is made of Christmas; but the public schools cannot use any holiday to teach the Christian religion as contrasted with Judaism or any other religion.

Religious Groups

The great religions agree in general upon the inherent worth and dignity of the individual, and emphasize brotherhood. They all have the Golden Rule and the Ten Commandments or their equivalent. The great religions acknowledge God and assert divine sanction for morality. Such fundamental values are not the exclusive possessions of any one religion. They belong to all mankind. These values are nonsectarian, but we divide sharply into sectarian groups when we define God and explain revelation.

The concept of God varies all the way from a personal living God to a philosophical ideal or First Cause. Some elevate the state or society to the level of God. If "God" is viewed merely as the ultimate source of values, and if religion be defined as our response to this ultimate, then statism, humanism, and secularism are themselves sectarian religions. They are so recognized and taught as theological points of view in schools of theology. The public schools have no more right to teach philosophical secularism than they have to teach any other sectarian religion.

In America all religious groups are minorities, or are divided into subgroups which are minorities. The rights of all minorities are respected, but no minority (and not even a majority) can force its religious beliefs or disbeliefs upon others through the public schools. For example, *atheists may disbelieve in God and may teach their children that there is no God. The public schools fully respect their rights, but atheists cannot require the public schools to teach atheism. The public schools cannot teach that the Declaration of Independence and our historic traditions are based upon a fallacy.*

Need for Defined Policy

Occasional abuses may occur in dealing with religion in the public schools, as they may happen also in treating politics. Necessary freedom implies some opportunity to make mistakes. But abuses occur less often when responsibility and acceptable procedures are defined. The right of the pupil to learn is not served by attempting to isolate the school from the community and the world, and forbidding any mention of things political or religious. School principals and teachers can better understand and more easily comply with policy when it is clearly defined and officially established in the community.

CONTROVERSIAL ISSUES

Most of the school curriculum is composed of established truths and accepted values that provoke no controversy. The American heritage and our established traditions are not controversial. But in a growing culture, social change is inevitable and the curriculum of the public schools includes the study of some unsolved problems which involve controversy.

Controversial issues result from conflicts in the cherished interests, beliefs, or affiliations of large groups of our citizens. Controversial issues arise in the important proposals or policies concerning which our citizens hold conflicting points of view. Controversial issues tend to separate political parties, management and labor, city and country, and other large groups of our people who disagree on public policy or proposed solutions to important problems.

Controversial issues are appropriately studied in the public schools insofar as the maturity of the pupils and the means available permit. Pupils in senior high schools are mature enough to study most of the significant controversial issues facing our citizens. Only through the study of such issues (political, economic, or social) does youth develop certain abilities required for American citizenship.

The schools do not "teach" controversial issues, but rather make suitable provision for pupils to "study" them. The schools teach the American heritage (our established truths and accepted values) and, in doing this, provide suitable opportunities for pupils, under competent guid-

ance, to study *inherent controversial issues. For example, the schools provide for the* study *of other philosophies and forms of government, such as the totalitarian government of communism and fascism. This is necessary to teach pupils thoroughly the values of American democracy. Pupils should know something of the competing philosophies and forms of government and the alternatives to our democratic way of life in order to acquire a deep and firm devotion to America based upon understanding. Conviction in the absence of understanding is little more than prejudice. It is less stable and more susceptible to successful attack.*

On all grade levels, therefore, the schools provide opportunities for pupils, according to their maturity, to analyze current problems, gather and organize pertinent facts, discriminate between fact and opinion, detect propaganda, identify prejudice, draw intelligent conclusions, respect the opinions of others, and accept the principles of majority rule and the rights of minorities. Free discussion of controversial issues, with free access to all relevant information, is the heart of the democratic process. Freedom of speech and free access to information are among our most cherished traditions.

Desirable policy on the study of controversial issues in the public schools is defined in terms of the rights of pupils rather than in terms of the rights of teachers. In the study of controversial issues, the pupil has four rights to be recognized:

1. The right to study any controversial issue which has political, economic, or social significance and concerning which (at his level) he should begin to have an opinion.

2. The right of free access to all relevant information, including any materials that circulate freely in the community.

3. The right to study under competent instruction in an atmosphere free from bias and prejudice.

4. The right to form and express his own opinion without jeopardizing his relation to his teacher or the school.

The treatment of controversial issues is objective and scholarly, with a minimum emphasis on opinion. The teacher approaches controversial issues in the classroom in an impartial and unprejudiced manner, and must refrain from using his teaching position and prestige to promote a partisan point of view. Good teaching of subjects containing important controversial issues requires more skill than most other kinds of teaching and, so far as possible, only teachers skilled in handling controversial issues are assigned to teach subjects which involve much controversy.

Instructional policy on controversial issues should be clearly defined and officially established in the community in order to insure youth a thorough and well-balanced preparation for American citizenship, and to protect teachers and school administrators from unwarranted attacks by pressure groups that may attempt to use the schools for partisan purposes.

THE CHALLENGE

Our country today is going through one of the most important periods in its history. We are in an era of rapid development and far-reaching worldwide change. We have much at stake. Easily undervalued in assessing our assets are the potentialities of our human resources. Of all our resources, our youth offer our greatest hope. The outcome will be determined finally by how well we utilize our capacity to learn, including our every resource of mind, of spirit, and of will.

If we are to meet in full strength whatever the future may bring, the schools of our country must not only attack their problems with vigor and deep insight but must also be better understood by the public that supports them. Their needs, the nature and scope of their activities, and how well they discharge their responsibilities are not now well understood. To achieve their maximum effectiveness the schools require not only the best in leadership, in facilities, and in personnel, but also a high level of community understanding and intelligent community support.

The schools welcome constructive criticism. Any citizen who seeks through genuine interest and honest inquiry to understand the purposes, program, and problems of his schools, and then seeks to influence constructively an improved performance of these functions, renders his schools and his community a valued service. But whoever fails to inform himself, and through false charges seeks to destroy confidence in the schools, does our country a great disservice.

American education is fundamentally sound. The instructional program is ever improving as the science and art of education develop, and as communities cooperate more helpfully with their educational agencies. If we take the long view, we must recognize that the growing generation is the most precious of our resources; that its competence, attitudes, and loyalties should be made our chief concern; and that its talents and abilities must be nurtured and developed to the utmost. Education is the most important opportunity, and the greatest responsibility, of every American community.

Section VI

THE ROLE OF SCIENCE AND RESEARCH: VALUES AND ISSUES[9]

Problems and Issues

Ten years ago the full development of the critical problems and issues now facing us could not be accurately predicted:
- Aging and geriatrics.
- Atomic war.
- Better allocation of resources to education, and better utilization of resources already available to the schools.
- Civil rights.
- Curriculum of greater breadth, in keeping with individual and social needs.
- Delinquency.
- Development of children and youth as the greatest resource of society.
- Disadvantaged children.
- Drugs.
- Economic interdependence within our own country and abroad.
- Educational leadership in serving the schools as the greatest opportunity and responsibility of society.
- "Explosion" of research knowledge, technology, and automation.
- Federal role in education and in support of innovations, and issues of decentralization.
- Greater interdependence between educational institutions and economic-social forces.
- Health.
- Housing.
- Integration and equality of opportunity.
- Jobs and unemployment.
- Leisure time.
- Negotiations and militant organizations of teachers.
- Population explosion.
- Poverty.
- Racial and militant minority groups.
- Religion in the school program as affected by court decisions and legislation.
- "Revolt" of the young.
- Sex.
- Urban school systems and inner-city children.
- Vocational education.

We may comment more specifically, by way of illustration, on a number of critical problems and issues now confronting the schools and society more broadly.

----

[9]Carter V. Good, *Essentials of Educational Research: Methodology and Design.* New York: Appleton-Century-Crofts, 1966. pp. 1-49.

The often harried superintendent (and his administrative team) must deal with increasingly militant organizations of teachers, pupils, parents, and other citizens who demand a voice in shaping policy. He is confronted with sanctions, strikes, work stoppages, and "professional" days. Many political leaders and others have adroitly related housing conditions, poverty, unemployment, delinquency, segregation, and other discriminatory practices to school policy and management, thus holding school administrators responsible for resolving social and economic problems not directly related to instruction.

School systems in both the North and the South have been shaken by racial problems and issues as militant minorities have pressed aggressively for equality of opportunity and fuller recognition in the total culture of society.

The school and our society now face the unfortunate fact that the "American heritage and our established traditions" (R) of merit are regarded by all too many persons as controversial in nature, thus posing major problems for the curriculum. Academic freedom has been greatly extended over the past decade. It is only accurate to say that the curriculum and teaching go considerably beyond "established truths and accepted values" (R), since development of skills and subjective statements by teachers now make up a considerable part of the program of instruction.

During recent years court decisions and legislation have greatly affected religious programs in the schools. It is generally recognized, however, that religion profoundly influences and contributes to society. It has been suggested that the school may develop an effective course in comparative religion.

As to special days in the school calendar, when effectively planned, they may serve to interpret our culture and subcultures.

Research and Science

As we deal with the urgent issues of today, some critics of research in the social sciences, particularly in the area of federally supported studies, have been forthright, but not wholly objective, in sweeping generalizations to the effect that such research should be more useful in solving major social problems, better coordinated, less slanted toward the accumulation of large bodies of facts, and better evaluated and publicized. According to these critics, social research emphasizing pursuit of knowledge for its own sake tends to be "trivial or irrelevant; usable, but not used; valuable, but buried in scholarly journals or government filing cabinets." Other criticisms of social investigations include undue emphasis on undirected, small-scale research proposed by individual investigators; too much quantitative analysis, which may actually prevent greater social understanding; imbalance between research on causes and on solutions and remedies; and the tendency of federal agencies to withhold findings that criticize present performance or policies.[10]

In evaluating the use of federal money in university research, there are some historic failures, and major political issues or problems, in which science is inescapably involved. We must learn to deal with these problems as follows:

1. To support an educational scientific establishment, including private as well as public institutions, without either destroying its freedom or leaving it in a position of privileged irresponsibility.

2. To fit the research interests of free scientists into a pattern of public policy and take account of the need for balanced national development, while building up our existing centers of high scientific quality.

3. To devote our knowledge to the service of human welfare as effectively as it has been enlisted in the service of national defense.

4. To make needed changes in some of our most stubborn political and administrative habits.[11]

The field of "human resources" has attracted a constantly increasing number of investigators, with interests in the various stages of the developmental process, family attitudes and environmental mores, attitudes and behavior of children with respect to the future, the learning process, man's education and his later performance in the world of work, and "investment in human capital," including the problems of race relations, poverty, the handicapped, the talented, crime, alcoholism, mental disease, desertion and divorce, gambling, and drug addition.[12]

Science is not enough, however, and calls on the philosopher for help in guiding the dreams of men, with philosophy "presenting its mission humbly and in the concepts that science offers." The "gentleman" of culture is a man with a mission "to minister to the welfare of the society in which he lives, and who takes a just pride in his guidance and his leadership." While we must abolish poverty, let us remember that man does not live by bread alone and that the greatest joy in life is that of accomplishment; "the spirit of man is best ministered to by giving him opportunity that is real and unfettered."[13]

[10]AHE College and University Bulletin 19:5; June 1, 1967. Based on a report prepared for the House Subcommittee on Research and Technical Programs.
[11]Don K. Price, "Federal Money and University Research." Science 151:285-90; January 21, 1966.
[12]Eli Ginzberg, The Development of Human Resources. New York: McGraw-Hill, 1966. x + 299 pp.
[13]Vannevar Bush, Science Is Not Enough. New York: William Morrow, 1967. 192 pp.

Science and Human Values

During recent years the interrelationships of science and public policy have been recognized as increasingly important, with major efforts on the part of government, philanthropic foundations, universities, and other research agencies to help science and technology serve the best interests of the nation. This view includes a place for the great humanities, the spiritual ends of life, faith, and values. The strength and integrity of science must be maintained in the face of varied opportunities, responsibilities, and distractions, including the involvement of scientists in social problems. Scientists are challenged to distinguish clearly between their conduct in science and behavior in dealing with issues that go beyond science alone. While the world of social and human affairs requires judgment and objectivity as essential elements in problem-solving, it also weighs opinions and pressures and compromises, as well as facts, in the attempt to make value judgments. We must combat the notions that science and engineering (or other technical fields) are incompatible with the great humanities or are narrowly materialistic and destructive of human values. The clear task of men of science is to face the future undeterred by the uncertainties of human survival. This faith in science is not incompatible with or exclusive of any other kind of faith, and indeed there is no inconsistency in considering scientific knowledge one of the great instruments of higher ends.[14]

Social Science and Values

The social sciences especially are concerned with values, including social decisions, interests, desires, beliefs, prejudices, and moral implications. The "hard-nosed" or "quantitative" social scientist seeks to avoid problems of policy, value preferences, and fact-value judgments. If he deals with such problems at all, it is in terms of incidence, distribution, and intensity, in a given population, with an objective and quantitative preoccupation. This value-free posture tends to blind the investigator to the really great problems of man and society, and may make social science the servant of any power elite that seeks to manipulate human behavior, regardless of goal or purpose. A value-free science is absurd in any strict sense, since science has its own norms or standards, and the search for truth or falsity is not unrelated to discovery of what is good or bad. Science may be good or bad in the degree it contributes to, or corresponds with, the basic needs and goals of human

---

[14]Alan T. Waterman, "The Changing Environment of Science." *Science* 147:13-18; January 1, 1965.

life. As both scientist and citizen, the social scientist may well seek to change those conditions of character and environment that interfere with rational choices between alternative modes of behavior. Attitudes of indifference or cynicism on the part of scientists toward moral and ethical problems of society can result in apathy and cynicism among other citizens, with resulting dangers to both science and a good society.[15]

Science and Moral-Social Responsibility

In general, the accomplishments of science in our time are almost miraculous, with the rate of progress still accelerating. Research can continue to expand as long as society is friendly toward this form of progress. There is evidence of stress and strain, however, between the great accomplishments of the physical sciences and the much slower development of the social sciences (which provide the controls for human behavior). At times an impossible course of action has been suggested, to the effect that physical research should take a holiday until social science catches up, since certain discoveries (as in the domain of atomic energy) involve the potential for great harm to, or even destruction of, society when wrongly applied. Scholars and scientists have a grave social obligation to see that scientific and technological (and social) discoveries are used for the benefit of society and that appropriate controls of human behavior are developed, with the aid of knowledge in social science, psychology, education, and religion. We constantly ask ourselves the haunting question: Can science aid in the search for sophistication in dealing with order and disorder in human affairs, not only to enrich individual lives but to prolong the survival of the human species in an acceptable form of society? While scientists and scholars must be free to establish the objectives of their research, the supporting society must be equally free to take account of its own needs. The union of intellectual power and moral concern or responsibility must be the foundation of both free science (and inquiry) and a just society.[16]

We may emphasize again that the great purpose of science is a better life for man, with research born of problems and man's determination to solve them. We must avoid the mistake, however, of imputing to science the qualities of "good" or "bad," since it is the *applications* that man makes of science and research which may be deeply moral and may fundamentally affect human welfare. In our search for "the good life" we make demands on many fields of science, including social science, and also enter the realm of values and religion. Social science and religion

---

[15]Peter H. Odegard, "The Social Sciences and Society." *Science* 145:1,127; September 11, 1964.
[16]Don K. Price, "J. Robert Oppenheimer." *Science* 155:1,061; March 3, 1967.

are complementary, in the sense that man has found many of his criteria for living in his religion, and in turn social research has contributed to religious thought.

To use the biological sciences as an example, biologists are well aware of the rapidly growing abilities of man to alter the face of the earth through the enormous physical power of technology, and they also know that such physical alterations can bring about far-reaching (and often destructive) changes in the life of our planet. We should not seek to overcome the natural world, but to live in harmony with it through learning how to control both the external environment and ourselves. Our basic interests concern the genetics and dynamics of populations, the factors that control biological productivity, the ways in which plants and animals and men adapt to their environment, and the changing distribution of living things in the sea and air, and on land.[17]

Social Science and Responsibility

Scientists can help overcome the uncertainty, confusion, and fear generated by the crises of war by presenting objectively and calmly the necessary facts to the public. The same call of duty that has placed science at the command of warfare now requires scientists and scholars to serve with equal devotion the social need for peace and find a means of protecting society that does not run the risk of destroying it. Governmental agencies are now placing more reliance on social science in determining public policy and in improving communication between social scientists and public officials.

We are reminded that in the past man's basic problems were concerned with the complexities of his physical environment, but now in our time the focus of the basic problem has changed from the external to the internal environment (notwithstanding outer space research). Our primary need is now to learn rapidly how to cope with ourselves and with each other, particularly with regard to intergroup and international conflicts, so that we can preserve freedom in peace. Does our future security depend as much upon priority in exploring outer space as upon our wisdom in managing the space in which we live? Is an inch forward in the realm of the mind worth a billion miles into outer space?

Much has been said about the social responsibility of the scientist, frequently meaning the physical scientist. The rapid increase of knowledge about the control of the physical world has posed the question of whether society will be able to direct this knowledge, applying it for the bene-

---

[17]Roger Revelle, "International Biological Program." *Science* 155:957; February 24, 1967.

fit of mankind rather than for the destruction of man and his civilization. The social responsibility of the social scientist is equally great in
the sense of discovering enough knowledge about society so that society
can, if it wishes to employ this information, control the use of physical
knowledge. The next question logically follows: Once the social scientists gain the social knowledge that is needed to control physical knowledge and society, how will this social evidence be controlled and .what
is to prevent a social scientist from taking advantage of such social
knowledge to expedite the enslavement or the destruction of society?
What is there to prevent one group in society from employing this social knowledge for the purpose of controlling another group? The social
scientist's activities should be an asset to democratic society and he
should be constantly alert to his obligation as a member of that society.

We have certain resources to use as a basis for meeting today's challenge to our schools and education more broadly: Descriptions of recent
changes in elementary-secondary schools and higher education, information about transformations in culture and society affecting education,
and at least an outline of the possible contributions of social and behavioral science to realization of individual and social goals. Such knowledge and techniques and values must be applied to the content and organization of the curriculum, to materials and methods of instruction,
and to organization and administration of the educational enterprise. In
dealing with our critical problems and issues now and in the years ahead
may we have the desire, evidence, sense of values, and wisdom to meet
the challenge of today and the future. May we have the time and repose
to do the things that need to be done.